That's My Buddy!

Friendship and Learning Across the Grades

Ideas from the
Child Development Project

DEVELOPMENTAL STUDIES CENTER

DEVELOPMENTAL STUDIES CENTER

2000 EMBARCADERO, SUITE 305
OAKLAND, CA 94606-5300
(800) 666-7270 / (510) 533-0213

That's My Buddy! is published by the Developmental Studies Center (DSC), an education nonprofit located in Oakland, California. At DSC we develop, evaluate, and disseminate programs that foster children's ethical, social, and intellectual development. While nurturing children's capacity to think skillfully and critically, we also strive to deepen children's commitment to prosocial values such as kindness, helpfulness, personal responsibility, and respect for others – qualities we believe are essential to leading humane and productive lives in a democratic society.

Funding to support the development, piloting, and dissemination of Developmental Studies Center programs has been provided by the following:

The Annenberg Foundation, Inc.

Anonymous Donor

Center for Substance Abuse Prevention, Substance Abuse and Mental Health Services Agency, U.S. Department of Health and Human Services

The Danforth Foundation

Evelyn and Walter Haas, Jr. Fund

The William and Flora Hewlett Foundation

The Robert Wood Johnson Foundation

The Walter S. Johnson Foundation

Ewing Marion Kauffman Foundation

W. K. Kellogg Foundation

John S. and James L. Knight Foundation

Lilly Endowment, Inc.

The John D. and Catherine T. MacArthur Foundation

A.L. Mailman Family Foundation, Inc.

National Science Foundation

Nippon Life Insurance Foundation

The Pew Charitable Trusts

The Rockefeller Foundation

Louise and Claude Rosenberg, Jr.

The San Francisco Foundation

The Spencer Foundation

Spunk Fund, Inc.

Stuart Foundations

Surdna Foundation, Inc.

DeWitt Wallace–Reader's Digest Fund, Inc.

CONTENTS

PREFACE

Community Counts

COMMON SENSE tells us that children learn best when they feel connected to their school – when school provides them with a warm and caring social context that we would characterize as "community." In fact, educational research supports this assumption, pointing to "community" as a predictor of students' ability to function successfully in school – both socially and academically – and to resist self-destructive behaviors such as drug and alcohol use.

Given this understanding of the importance of community, what can elementary schools do to help students feel connected to their school? A Buddies program is surely one approach. When children are given opportunities to develop caring, trusting friendships across grade levels, when these friendships center around shared learning experiences that are engaging for both older and younger students, and when students see that their teachers have buddies too, the concept of community is experienced, not just idealized.

What is special about the Buddies program described here is not just that students of different ages work together. What makes this Buddies program special are the *purposes* for which we advocate cross-age experiences and the *kinds* of learning experiences that we want students to share. When a Buddies program is explicitly focused on building school community and sharing learning experiences that are noncompetitive and open-ended, what we find are children who feel good about themselves and good about each other.

That's My Buddy! has grown out of the experiences of hundreds of teachers and children in schools in San Ramon, Hayward, Salinas, Cupertino, and San Francisco, California; Louisville, Kentucky; Miami and Homestead, Florida; and White Plains, New York – all of whom have been working with the Child Development Project (CDP) over the past decade to build caring communities in their schools. Research conducted in these schools during this period points to the following important components of a school community in which students and adults care about learning and about each other:

- stable, warm relationships
- teaching for understanding
- a challenging, learner-centered curriculum
- simultaneous focus on intellectual, ethical, and social development
- close cooperation between families and school staff.

The Buddies program described in this book is just one aspect of the CDP program, which offers a range of professional development experiences and curriculum and instructional materials (see page 139) that incorporate constructivist learning theory, cooperative learning techniques, class-room and schoolwide community-building strategies, and an approach to classroom management that helps students develop self-control and a commitment to fundamental values such as fairness, kindness, and responsibility.

Eric Schaps, President of the Developmental Studies Center, and Marilyn Watson, Program Director of the Child Development Project, have provid-ed the vision and leadership for CDP, and have made it possible for the ideas in *That's My Buddy!* to become widely available. Amy Schoenblum and Rosa Zubizarreta were the creative team that researched and devel-oped this resource, with invaluable contributions from teachers and students in CDP schools across the country. Sylvia Kendzior led a team of staff developers who helped teachers experiment with Buddies in their classrooms. Lynn Murphy was the book's editor and Kathryn Chetkovich gave it polish. Photographs were taken from videotapes produced by Peter Shwartz, and desktop publishing and art direction were provided by Allan Ferguson and Visual Strategies. Ginger Schiffer provided editorial support. Our special "buddy artists" are Ethan and Rhiannon Guevin, Eric and Mark Lammerding, Raisa Lee, Maggie Wong, and Zachary Zilber.

We would like to thank everyone who contributed their ideas to this pub-lication, especially the teachers who shared their Buddies stories and invited us into their classrooms and schools — Rosie Alvarez, Dorothy Birley, Sandy Boyd, Michele Alsterlind Brynjulson, Laurel Cress, Lynn Dames, Cynthia Evans, Maureen Jackson, Melody Lane, Louise Lotz, Becky O'Bryan, Vic Paglia, Gail Peluso, Phil Plummer, Linda Rayford, Randi Sack, Margie Ura, Maria Vallejo, Anne Weaver, and Linda Yamasaki. Thank you, all.

How to Use This Book

THAT'S MY BUDDY! begins with an overview of Buddies and an in-depth look at the social and academic benefits it offers children, teachers, and entire school communities. All of this can be found in **Part 1: Why Do Buddies? A Rationale.**

Part 2: Getting Started with Other Teachers offers ideas and strategies for everything you need to know to get started with Buddies in your school. Whether your entire school community is getting involved or you are piloting Buddies with only one other teacher, you can get practical ideas about how to establish teacher partnerships, how to frame your initial planning, and what to consider in putting student pairs together. (We've also provided several resources in Part 5 to support your planning.)

Part 3: Making It Work with Students provides suggestions about how to prepare students for a Buddies program and introduce the pairs for the first time, how to introduce each activity, and how to give students many opportunities to share and reflect on their experiences. You'll also find a few tried-and-true hints from teachers and troubleshooting suggestions for common problems that might arise as students are getting used to Buddies.

Part 4: Activity Ideas is where you'll find examples of activities that have been piloted in Child Development Project schools around the country. GETTING TO KNOW YOU activities help children get to know their buddies and feel comfortable with one another. LEARNING TOGETHER activities can be integrated into existing academic programs to support your learning goals for both older and younger students. STEPPING OUT activities take buddy pairs out of the classroom and suggest a variety of new experiences and new environments for them to explore together. Finally, CELEBRATING OUR YEAR activities give children an important opportunity to thank and appreciate their buddies, and to reflect on what they have learned together throughout the year.

Part 5: Resources is a collection of planning and evaluation tools that may be useful as you initiate and carry out a Buddies program in your classroom or school. We encourage you to photocopy any of these resources as often as you need.

PART 1

Why Do Buddies?
A Rationale

ANYONE who spends time in schools understands how complex children's social relationships are and how crucial they are to students' overall liking for school. A Buddies program is a powerful way to help *all* children experience positive social relationships and enjoy a fresh perspective on themselves as learners. Because a Buddies program is structured by pairing students in classes of "big" kids with students in classes of "little" kids, it transcends the usual age-mate pecking order that often leaves some children feeling inadequate or excluded. Buddy partnerships allow the older students to experience themselves as caring, competent, and valued, while the younger students can experience themselves as worthy of special attention and kindness. Everyone wins, and reciprocal exclamations of "That's my buddy!" make the whole school a friendlier, warmer place.

The friendlier, warmer part goes for teachers, too. According to the teachers we interviewed for this book, it's fun to have a buddy, and the partnership that two buddy teachers model for their classes has a way of strengthening the adult community in the school as well.

No matter what your motivation in trying a Buddies program – to complement a schoolwide commitment to building community, to vary children's learning experiences, or to address a particular problem like teasing or bullying – we hope this resource supports your efforts.

" *I do Buddies because the impact on my children is so profound – you can see the effects on the playground and throughout the whole school."*

....

" *I think some children come to school on certain days just so they can go to Buddies."*

....

" *The kids love Buddies, and they love seeing the familiar faces of their buddies in the hall. They really feel like they're part of an extended school family."*

....

Relationships

Creating Intentional Caring Relationships

If we tell children, "Let's all be nice to each other," or "It's nice to help others," or "Please don't pick on little children," they may hear and repeat these norms, but they may not be able to act on them.

Instead of exhortations alone, children need real opportunities to practice helping and caring for others and to experience being part of a community built upon these values. When children of different ages have a chance to get to know one another, learn from each other, and have fun together in a safe and supportive environment, they are likely to value their friendship and the way it makes them feel. A successful buddy friendship lets children know they are capable of building relationships and showing care — and it can provide the motivation for them to create similar relationships with other children, family members, and adults throughout the school community.

Teachers have found that as a result of Buddies, they see more spontaneous helping behavior and less teasing, which contributes to a schoolwide atmosphere of trust. A trusting atmosphere, in turn, supports children's further development as caring, principled individuals. Many teachers say that as a result of a Buddies program, their school communities feel completely different now — more like "extended families." They tell us that the children feel a greater sense of belonging, and in some cases children come to school on certain days just so they can participate in Buddies!

Redefining "Cool"

" It keeps you soft when you're around people who are vulnerable in some way."

When a Buddies program takes hold, it helps to address many of the social barriers that exist because of grade-level grouping. Without a Buddies program most children have few opportunities to interact and develop caring friendships with older or younger children in their school. And when they do interact, older children are not always kind and helpful to those who are younger and smaller.

In some schools the age segregation that comes with grade-level grouping (and that children commonly impose on themselves) is reinforced by school policies. For example, the logistics of dealing with a crowded lunchroom may require "staggered" lunch and recess blocks, which typically are scheduled by age groups. Sometimes decisions that result in age separation are intended to "protect" the younger and older children from each other. What often results, no matter what the reason for the age separation, is the stereotyping of older children as "intimidating" and younger children as "pesty."

What's even more troubling is that older children, especially, often earn their negative reputation by taking unfair advantage of their status as older, bigger, and more experienced. We see this when older children use more than their share of the play area or equipment, make certain sections of the bus "off-limits" to little kids, and tease and intimidate younger children just for "fun." Younger children quickly learn to acquiesce to their older and more "experienced" schoolmates.

" *Buddies makes me much more patient with my younger brothers and sisters at home. When I get home and they're bugging me, now I know they just want my attention, and I try to spend some time with them."*

— FIFTH-GRADER,
LOUISVILLE, KENTUCKY

◀ *When children know someone younger is counting on them, it brings out their best caretaking instincts.*

But what if young children could experience their older schoolmates as kind, caring, and trustworthy? What if we could help older children feel that it's not only respectable but "cool" to be kind and caring rather than tough and bossy? Peer pressure is powerful, and it needn't be negative. By emphasizing that it's OK to be kind, helpful, and supportive to younger children, a Buddies program allows children to "fit in" while they also act in ways they know are right and fair.

Academics

Reinforcing a Learning Orientation

If you're wondering how you can spend time on building relationships without sacrificing valuable academic time, take heart.

Buddies is designed to *support* your academic goals for students, not take time away from them. One of the strongest messages of a Buddies program is that we're all learners and learning can be fun.

Focusing on Process, Not Product

Three kinds of learning experiences are well suited to a Buddies program: rehearsal, scaffolding, and open-ended discovery. What makes each successful is the role it provides for both older and younger students to be active learners.

Rehearsal activities are tied closely to particular classroom learning activities in which buddies use each other as a resource for reporting, rehearsing, or practicing. For example, buddies can be each other's audience for learning reports – personal "what-I-learned-this-week" reflections (that also then go home) – or for sharing information or questions in a research report, or for appreciating the selection each has made from his or her learning portfolio. Buddies can also help each other practice particular

> 66 *With my students I see the increased responsibility, not only for their own learning, but for what they're supposed to be giving to their buddy or helping their buddy along with."*

skills they are trying to master, rehearse a presentation, or memorize specific classroom content. In rehearsal activities, buddies provide each other with a receptive audience or an interactive sounding board.

A second approach to buddy learning is to structure activities in which the older buddies scaffold the learning of their younger buddies by acting as the more knowledgeable and experienced learner. One of the best ways for children to consolidate what they are learning is to teach someone else. Teaching their buddies gives older children a chance not only to celebrate what they know, but also to learn by explaining. Older children are able to grapple with the question of how to translate what they have learned so that it will be appropriate for their younger buddies – a consideration that brings them deeper into their subject *and* into how people learn. For example, older students who read with their buddies can sharpen their own reading strategies as they help their buddies try to figure out an unfamiliar word, an unstated assumption, or a connection to their own experience. And, obviously, younger children also benefit as learners from this kind of one-on-one attention.

A third way buddies can help each other meet academic goals is through open-ended activities designed to engage each learner in different ways or at different levels. So, for example, buddy pairs could play a dice game in which one child is learning about probability while the other learns to tally and chunk numbers. Or buddies could create their own books in which one student acts primarily as the author and the other as the illustrator. Or, as another alternative, buddies could make field notes about a neighborhood walk and then explain which things each of them found most interesting and why. In open-ended activities, as in rehearsal and scaffolding activities, the most important learning

" *To me, the easiest part of teaching has been having the buddies together. It's not just the caring and the loving, but also how to help another person academically. When we come together, I have 28 other teachers in here."*

goal is that students present themselves to each other as learners and support each other in that role.

Everybody Wins

How Do Older Children Benefit?

Although both older and younger children benefit from having a buddy, many teachers say that the impact on older children is the more powerful. When you ask students to be older buddies, you send the message: "I think you're mature, I think you have a lot to offer as role models for younger people, and I think you are able to handle responsibility well."

As role models, older buddies develop an understanding of what it means to have younger children look up to them. Many take their buddy responsibility very seriously, acting with unusual patience and

It feels good to know a younger child thinks you're terrific. ▼

understanding. As they interact with their younger buddies, they are able to recognize their own maturity and to remember that they once (not too long ago) were small. Most older buddies use their power to shape the buddy relationship in ways that show genuine concern for the smaller child in their care. Buddy relationships also give older children the opportunity to practice treating others the way they would like to be treated, and to experience the satisfaction that comes with that.

The benefits of a buddy relationship for older children cluster around the ways they can experience their own growth, the ways they can experience themselves as contributing to the growth of someone else, and the ways the relationship pushes them to continue growing.

> *I've always wanted a little sister. Now it's like I've got one and I can help her do things, and it feels like we are closer than friends would be. I'm giving more to her than I'd give to other people, and I just feel really special that I can do that for her."*
>
> — FIFTH-GRADER,
>   LOUISVILLE, KENTUCKY

WAYS OLDER BUDDIES BENEFIT

- **Experience themselves as responsible**
- **Experience themselves as caring**
- **See themselves as valuable "helpers" who contribute toward the welfare of others**
- **Feel important and appreciated in someone else's life**
- **Draw on their own life experiences in guiding others**
- **Make social connections and "fit in" in ways they might not with peers**
- **Experience themselves as learners**
- **Gain insight into the challenges of being a "teacher"**
- **Have fun!**

Your role in supporting older students to meet the challenges of working with younger children is pivotal in helping them build strong self-concepts that can carry over into their other schoolwork and their other relationships.

How Do Younger Children Benefit?

Younger children can develop a growing sense of belonging and security through a Buddies program. A Buddies program helps all children feel part of an extended school family, but this is especially true for younger children. In turn, when young children feel they are part of a caring community, they are likely to develop a stronger commitment to treating others with respect, care, and appreciation.

The beauty of Buddies is that children experience both sides of the relationship — first as a younger buddy, and later as an older buddy. Children are able

" It's fun to have a buddy because it's like you have a friend with you all the time."

— FIRST-GRADER, LOUISVILLE, KENTUCKY

Special attention from an older buddy inducts young children into the school norms for kindness and learning. ▼

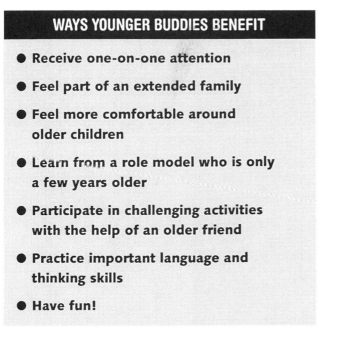

WAYS YOUNGER BUDDIES BENEFIT

- **Receive one-on-one attention**

- **Feel part of an extended family**

- **Feel more comfortable around older children**

- **Learn from a role model who is only a few years older**

- **Participate in challenging activities with the help of an older friend**

- **Practice important language and thinking skills**

- **Have fun!**

to see their own growth over time, develop a greater appreciation of the benefits and responsibilities that can be enjoyed as they grow up, and remember with increased empathy, perhaps, what it's like to be small.

How Do Hard-to-Reach Students Benefit?

Teachers say that a buddy relationship can be a breakthrough experience for hard-to-reach students, especially those who are in the position of being the older buddy. In such a relationship, children who are "outsiders" can find a comfortable, "insider's" place for themselves. For example, students who are disruptive and consistently alienate their peers can feel accepted by a younger buddy and relieved of a burdensome reputation. With a younger buddy, it's OK to be helpful, it's OK to be caring, and it's OK to be responsible. Similarly, older students who are shy or feel left out or isolated from

" *Michael. It was the only time I liked him. He was a very hard student to like, and I don't say that about many kids. He was very down on himself and was determined not to be liked. He told me the first week of school, 'Don't even bother, because you're going to kick me out faster than anybody else has.' But he was a very different person working with his little buddy. There were no preconceived notions from this younger child. Michael was able to be childlike and to let go of the hard piece of himself. He just melted. He had a little girl as a buddy and he was delightful."*

"We have children who have not been as successful academically at school. But having little buddies to help has made these students feel just like they're teachers. There's no competition and they're working at their own level. I think it has helped these students just feel so good about themselves, and their self-esteem has risen dramatically."

their peers have a chance to connect with someone who is younger and less threatening — and who looks up to them, even.

In schools where some students are chosen for an "advanced" program, teachers say that Buddies can be a valuable social experience. Children who learn quickly or learn at an advanced pace may be frustrated by others who don't know something they know, or who have a harder time learning. Buddies gives the most able students practice teaching others — and doing it with kindness and patience.

Students who have special academic needs also have a unique opportunity to grow in a buddy relationship. When paired with a younger buddy, these children are likely to be more competent than the younger child and able to teach and support that child. Being in such a leadership role can give a huge boost to a struggling student's self-esteem.

With a caring role model, ▶ *children can learn simple rules about classroom behavior and complex attitudes about their relationship to school.*

Benefits for the Teacher

Teachers are usually quick to see that a Buddies program supports their academic goals and the development of a caring classroom community; and, because Buddies can provide a different perspective on students, it may also allow teachers to appreciate and enjoy their students in new ways.

In a practical sense, Buddies helps teachers manage out-of-the-classroom excursions – around the building or around the town. Field trips, school assemblies, and even Halloween parades can be more easily managed when older buddies, themselves on their best behavior, are there to answer their younger buddies' questions and help them with self-control.

In addition, working closely with another teacher gives buddy teachers a chance to share ideas, learn from each other, take risks neither might have taken otherwise, build on individual strengths, and enjoy the companionship of another adult.

Benefits for the Whole School

Buddies is a community builder. When an entire school commits itself to Buddies, it sends the message, "Relationships are important." Building a caring community is seen as a clear priority. A Buddies program can create an exciting energy in a school and have a huge impact on how it feels to be there. We hope you'll try Buddies and let us know if you agree!

" It's that time together in that classroom, the 30–45 minutes each week that we spend together watching the kids and talking about teaching. Sometimes as a teacher you just don't get that kind of time, and I don't think it would have happened if we hadn't started this."

PART 2
Getting Started with Other Teachers

WHETHER your whole school has decided to try Buddies or you are partnering with another teacher on your own, it's always nice to get started early in the year. Buddies can be a lot of fun, but it also takes some time to plan and work together. Teachers who have done Buddies in the past recommend setting aside time to sit down with your partner and establish shared understandings regarding expectations, goals, and how communication will take place.

We hope that the following suggestions will assist you in laying this essential groundwork and in developing a successful Buddies program in your classrooms and school.

Starting Buddies on Your Own

If your whole school is not ready to commit to a yearlong Buddies program, take heart. Buddies is fairly simple to introduce on your own, as long as you have one other teacher who is willing to do it with you. You may want to ask someone you know or have worked with before, especially if this is your first time trying Buddies. Yet even this may not be necessary, as long as you are both truly interested in the project and willing to dedicate some time to planning and ongoing communication and reflection.

Once you've started Buddies, it's likely that other colleagues will be curious about what you're doing, and that interest in learning about it will spread throughout the school. If you see yourself as an "ambassador" for a schoolwide Buddies program, you may want to keep a portfolio for samples of the children's work and a journal for anecdotes and stories, your ideas and reflections, classroom observations, and anything else that may be useful in the future. This collection can be an excellent resource as you share your experiences with others at your

“ Even without schoolwide support, Buddies grows on you, and it grows on the whole school. Over time, as teachers recognize its value, they'll want to be included.”

school. The materials you collect may also be valuable if you make presentations about Buddies to parents, teacher groups, or administrators, or if you are working on any personal writing or research projects.

So, if you are on your own, find a partner and go for it! The rewards are many and are likely to spread beyond the two classes involved.

(*Note:* If you and a partner are working on your own, you may want to skim or skip the following section on starting a schoolwide program and proceed directly to "Initial Planning with Your Buddy Teacher," page 23.)

It can take only two buddy classrooms to kindle schoolwide enthusiasm for a Buddies program. ▼

Starting Buddies as a Schoolwide Program

If the entire school has decided to try Buddies, begin early in the school year with a schoolwide planning meeting. Ideally, teachers in your school will be familiar with Buddies from having participated in the decision to introduce it throughout the school. Whatever the general understanding of Buddies may be, it's helpful if everyone has the opportunity to explore a copy of this book before the schoolwide planning meeting. This way all teachers can be prepared to discuss the suggestions in the book, to share ideas, and to raise questions. You may also want to show the videotape *That's My Buddy!* – a 13-minute overview of Buddies programs in four pairs of classrooms.

Planning for Inclusiveness

One important function of a schoolwide planning meeting is to consider how to make your Buddies program as inclusive as possible. You may want to discuss how to include students who participate in special education classes (which may be significantly smaller than other classes or already cross-aged) or how to accommodate students with special needs who spend a substantial amount of time in pull-out programs. Consider, too, how to involve specialists who work with your students, as they may want to be a part of the Buddies experience as well. Discuss whatever seems important in making Buddies as inclusive as possible, and invite all teachers to participate in sharing ideas and making decisions.

Forming Teacher Partnerships

For teachers, Buddies is an opportunity to work together, to learn from each other, and to extend the walls of the classroom – in the context of a mutually supportive relationship. Although it's always nice to

"As a teacher, I like having the older children come down because I can see them learning and developing. Watching the older children, I get to see where my children will be in four years, and to see how what we do now is part of the process of helping them develop into the next stages. We're preparing them to be upper-grade students one day, and that means children who are problem-solvers, who are self-motivated 'teachers,' and who are caring and respectful of others."

When their buddy teachers ▶
trust and respect each other,
children have a powerful
model for their own buddy
relationships.

work with someone you already know, many teachers have been pleasantly surprised by partnerships that were selected randomly. For many, the opportunity to work with someone new has brought unique challenges and great rewards.

No matter how you form teacher partnerships, it is ideal for buddy classrooms to be at least three grade levels apart, such as kindergarten and third grade, first and fourth grades, and second and fifth grades. Teachers who have experimented with different combinations say that the greater the age difference between older and younger buddies, the better. A number of third-grade classes have enjoyed being older buddies to kindergartners and younger buddies to sixth-graders at the same time. If this is possible in your school, you may want to give it a try.

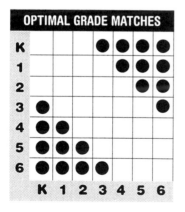

If your school has "combined" classes, it may mean that students in a two- or three-grade range are matched with students in a single grade (for example, a K–1–2 combination matched with a fifth grade), or it may mean that two combined classes are matched (for example, a K–1 combination matched with a 3–4 combination).

Given the ideal of separating buddy classes by at least three grade levels, here are a few suggestions about setting up the teacher partnerships themselves. As you consider the options, weigh the benefits and burdens of each as they apply to your school.

Teachers Choose. One of the best ways to create teacher partnerships is to respect individual choice and invite teachers to decide for themselves. Teachers can choose a colleague or friend they feel comfortable with — most likely someone with whom they share a teaching philosophy and approach to working with children. When buddy teachers start out with common understandings, they can jump in quickly to explore the program's potential.

One of the drawbacks when teachers choose someone they already know is that they miss an opportunity to get to know someone new or to stretch themselves beyond what is already familiar. Sometimes when teachers choose their own partners, established social cliques may be perpetuated and hurt feelings may result. Some teachers could feel left out or be forced to scramble at the last minute to find a partner.

Random Matching. Another option is to select partners randomly within predetermined grade levels (for instance, the kindergarten and first-grade teachers could pick names out of a hat that contains only the names of all the third- and fourth-grade teachers). Many teachers have told us about "unlikely" partnerships that came together through a process of random matching and ended up surprising everyone by how well they worked.

A random approach maximizes teachers' opportunities to work with colleagues they might not initially have chosen. It sends a message to everyone that it's important to be able to work collaboratively with all kinds of people — the very same message that we value in the classroom. Furthermore, if you decide

"We would never have gotten to know how much we have in common if it wasn't for doing Buddies. The more we've gotten to know each other through Buddies, the more we can see that we're alike in many ways — for example, in our dedication to our jobs, in the way we both worry and care deeply about the kids, and in the way we try to communicate with both children and parents."

to choose names randomly (once they are sorted by grade level), you may find yourself pleased to discover a growing collaborative spirit among all of the staff.

Drawbacks of a random approach include the possibility that teachers will feel that they have fewer choices in their work environment and fewer opportunities to work closely with their friends on the staff. The importance you attach to these drawbacks depends on the culture of your particular school and how teachers see their role in decision-making.

Through a Representative. If your school has very strong and supported grade-level teams, you may want to involve them in the matching process. For example, teachers could indicate their partner preferences to a colleague they have selected to represent their particular grade-level team. These representatives then meet to consider and recommend partnerships.

For this approach to work, it's important for teachers to understand that while an effort will be made to accommodate their preferences, other considerations may have to take precedence. This approach has the advantage of allowing for more teacher choice than random matching, but it also carries the risk of some teachers feeling unhappy with the resulting partnerships.

Through the Principal. If teachers are comfortable with the process, the principal could serve as the matchmaker in the same way that grade-level representatives might. Teachers could indicate several preferences and the principal would try to accommodate as many people as possible.

No matter what approach you choose or invent for matching buddy teachers, keep in mind that what's most important is for teachers to feel included in an authentic and deliberate decision-making process *before* the matching takes place.

> **"** *Trust and respect are what are really important. If you've built a sense of trust with the other person, then all things are possible."*

Initial Planning with Your Buddy Teacher

Teachers who have worked with Buddies stress the importance of adequate planning time at the beginning, and how well it pays off once the process is set in motion. Much of the work involved in Buddies is "front-end" work: establishing common goals and expectations, deciding how often you'll meet and the kinds of activities you'll do, and forming the children's buddy partnerships. We encourage you to take some time to focus on all three of these areas — as well as on getting to know each other better — in order to create a strong foundation for yourselves and the children. The more the children are able to see that the two of you are "buddies" who work together as a team, the more committed they will be to their own partnerships.

Teachers who invest time in planning for Buddies make the whole experience more pleasurable — for everyone.
▼

Sharing Goals and Expectations

It is particularly important to share your goals and expectations with your buddy teacher, along with any concerns that each of you may have. For example, do you both agree that the older buddies should not see themselves simply as tutors for the younger children? Are you both comfortable with activities that may not lead to a concrete product? Are you both committed to saving time for student reflection at the end of each buddy meeting?

You may also want to talk about some of your personal skills or interests that could be resources in your work together. For example, one of you may play the guitar or love working with papier-mâché; one of you may know a lot about tide pools or problem solving with math manipulatives. One of you may actually enjoy making arrangements or taking care of details.

A simple way to get all your concerns and ideas on the table is to begin your first planning meeting with a reciprocal "interview" (see "Goal Setting for Teacher Partnerships" on page 133 in the Resources section). This interview structure can help you establish some basic understandings about Buddies and explore each other's vision of your partnership.

When to Meet

One of the first decisions you will want to make is how often (and when) you want students to meet with their buddies. Teachers most commonly choose to meet on a weekly basis, though some choose to meet once a month. There are benefits to both schedules.

Teachers who prefer to start slowly with Buddies have their classes meet once a month – the minimum schedule if children are to develop relationships and a sense of continuity. Teachers who meet once a month often focus on "special" activities that take a bit more planning and time than do weekly activities. For example, once-a-month buddies may work on a special art, music, or drama project together, take a field trip together, attend a performance together, or do a community service project either within the school or outside in the greater community.

Many teachers who begin with a monthly schedule find themselves moving to a weekly schedule. Most teachers feel that the benefits of the program really take hold with weekly meetings. Not only do the children become more comfortable with each other, but the time they spend together becomes more integrated into the curriculum, as well as being something special to look forward to every week.

Teachers who bring students together weekly tend to plan activities that are easy to organize. Weekly activities are likely to have a predictable or regular quality – such as reading together, sharing learning, having lunch together, singing songs, etc. Once students learn the routines and procedures for these activities, they can become responsible for carrying out much of the activity on their own. And there's always room for the "special" activities that may take more time or planning.

Another benefit of a weekly schedule is that teachers and students can focus more on the buddy relationships than on the logistics of a particular activity or event. When students are settled into a routine, you have more time for observing and working with individual buddy pairs and for helping students reflect as a group about what they are learning, what is going well, and what can be improved.

What to Do

After you've decided on an initial schedule, you may want to choose some of the activities you will do together during the year. In making your initial selections, be sure to start with several getting-to-

"We meet once a week on Fridays. But I remember in my last school I had a buddy class and we kind of sporadically got together, so the bonding that's happened in our classrooms this year didn't happen then."

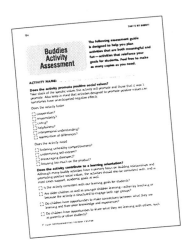

know-you activities. Look through the suggested activities on page 51 for some ideas; you'll see a repeated focus on relationship building as well as academic learning, and on reflection as well as action.

If you decide to create your own activities or adapt those presented here, you may find it helpful to refer to the design criteria provided in the "Buddies Activity Assessment," on page 134 in the Resources section. The activity assessment will help you focus on whether an activity promotes positive social values, a learning orientation, active engagement for both groups, and time to reflect.

No matter what activities you plan, be prepared for spontaneous suggestions from the children. The more that children have the opportunity to contribute to and take responsibility for their buddy experience, the better. Don't be surprised if you're subjected to a regular chorus of "We could do *that* with our buddies!"

Depending on the buddy activity and the size of your classes, you will also need to decide whether to keep the two classes together in one room, find a bigger all-purpose room, or use both of your classrooms. If buddies are going to snuggle together to share a book, there's probably room for everyone in one classroom. If they need space to assemble projects or rehearse skits, you may want to use an all-purpose room or both classrooms. If you have large classes and small rooms, find a way for each whole class to host the other at least some of the time.

Creating Student Partnerships

In addition to deciding how often buddies will meet and what they'll do, you and your buddy teacher will want to discuss and decide how to create the student partnerships. Many teachers pair students deliberately, with an explicit goal of meeting each

◀ *Since there's no one right way to match buddies, think hard about which way is best for you and your students.*

child's needs and interests. Others match students randomly for the year and support the children in working out any differences they may have. Some teachers do a combination of deliberate and random pairing, and still others have been able to include students directly in the process. The approaches presented below are those that teachers have found useful. We encourage you to weigh the benefits and burdens of each approach for your particular circumstances.

❝ *I match buddies carefully. We're talking about a relationship that's going to last all year – it needs to be able to ride out the bumps. On the other hand, I see a lot of benefits to using random grouping for cooperative groups, where your goal is to have children learn to work with everyone else."*

Deliberate Matching

The biggest reason teachers match students deliberately is to provide each student with a "good fit." These same teachers may prefer the egalitarianism of random grouping for classroom cooperative learning activities yet feel that since buddies stay together all year, it's important that they be carefully matched. Also, since buddies meet together for only 30 to 60 minutes each week (and some meet only once a month), these teachers feel it's best not to spend too much of this time working out personality differences between buddies.

If you and your partner decide to deliberately match your students, remember that you'll need to wait until a few weeks into the school year to begin. This way, each of you will have had the opportunity to get to know your students better. In preparation for matching buddies, you may want to take a few minutes to think about the following: Are any students particularly shy? Are any very outgoing? Who has a tendency to be unfocused or off-task, and what kind of partner might be a good match for this student? Do we have any students with learning difficulties or physical disabilities (see page 30)? Who appears to be very nurturing and likely to work well with a buddy who needs a little extra help?

You will find that as you and your partner begin to share impressions of your students, possible combinations will emerge. This process is also an excellent way for you to learn a little more about each other's students before the two classes meet.

Inviting Students to Participate in Matching

A number of teachers have invited students to participate in the process of forming buddy partnerships. Children are likely to have acquaintances of different ages from their neighborhood, church or temple, afterschool program, or other setting. Buddies can be an opportunity for children to deepen these acquaintances into friendships.

One way to include student participation is to show your students a list of names from the class with which they will be partnering and ask them to write down the name of anyone they know and would like to work with — making it very clear that while any request will be considered, there is no guarantee that it will be granted. (And reassure students that they are not expected to know anyone on the list.) The purpose is simply to enable children who do have a preference to make it known to the teacher.

66 *When an older child came midyear from India speaking very little English, I was unsure about which of my first-graders to match her with. So I decided to open it up to the kids. I asked my students if there was anybody who would be interested in working with a new student who spoke very little English. One student's hand shot up, and she was delighted to have the special job and the experience. They were wonderful together."*

While teachers generally create deliberate matches for students with special needs, there may be times when you want to solicit student input by asking for a volunteer to work with a particular student. Asking the children directly how best to match that child gives them the opportunity to make important choices for themselves about taking on extra responsibility. (See also the discussion of deliberately matching students with special needs, page 30.)

Matching Students Randomly

Some teachers believe strongly in matching students randomly. Just as adults need to be able to work with all kinds of people, children, too, benefit from learning to work with all kinds of peers. Furthermore, not every teacher finds it comfortable to "socially engineer" the situation, or to decide who is "best" for whom. Teachers who match students randomly are willing to accept conflicts or misunderstandings between buddies as part of the learning process and to support students in finding a way to work through and resolve them (this is desirable, of course, no matter how buddies are matched).

◀ *No matter how your buddies have been matched, they'll welcome your interest and support.*

If you decide to match students randomly, consider letting students know why you are doing it this way. Let students know that you want them to be able to work with all kinds of people, not just their best friends or people who share their interests or personality characteristics.

Random matching, like any other method for matching buddies, happens once at the beginning of the year, not each time buddies meet or begin a new project. No matter what initial matching process you use, the goal is to build long-term, supportive relationships – which is difficult to achieve if children switch buddies.

Combining Random and Intentional Matching

You may want to combine random and intentional matching, since both options have their advantages. Consider intentional matching for some of your students, such as those with special needs or challenges. On the other hand, when you either don't know a child well or don't have an informed opinion about whom he or she should work with, match randomly.

Students with Special Needs

Buddies is a great way to include students of all abilities, including those with disabilities and special needs. Everyone benefits from having a special relationship with an older or younger friend. When all students are fully included, children are also more likely to learn important lessons – that everyone is important, everyone has something to offer, everyone likes having friends, and everyone likes being treated with kindness and respect.

Most often, you will want to create deliberate matches for students with special needs. These may include children who are extremely shy or those with limited English proficiency, learning disabili-

◀ The more inclusive your Buddies program can be, the more everyone will benefit.

ties, physical and/or emotional challenges, or any of a number of conditions that in most situations set them apart from their peers. Talk with your partner about these students, and what kinds of buddy partners might be most appropriate, supportive, and able to handle the challenges and rewards of working with such a student.

If your special needs student has an attendant or classroom aide, include this adult in some of your planning and, of course, in all buddy activities. Similarly, you may want to involve the full-inclusion or special education specialist in your planning.

When the Special Needs Student Is Younger. Most teachers say they choose particularly nurturing, kind, and caring older buddies for younger children who have special needs. If you have a child with a severe impairment, you may want to talk with the older buddy ahead of time, offer some information, and give him or her a chance to ask you questions. Let the student know that you are available for support and assistance, and that you will check in with the buddies often.

When the Special Needs Student Is Older. The situation is obviously a little different if you have an upper-grade student with a disability or special

" *I carefully matched Jason, a mentally retarded fourth-grader, with Sam, a first-grader. After the first few buddy activities, Sam said to me, 'This year, it's more like I'm his buddy.' He felt proud to be able to help out, but I also wanted to reassure him that he wasn't on his own, and so I simply said, 'Yes, you might have noticed that Jason is a little different. We're going to make sure that Zachary and Andrew are always there with you guys.'"*

"Isaac was an older buddy to one of my first-graders last year. He knew that he had the toughest little one, a child who needed a lot of extra help. But we trusted him. Early this year he came down to see me after school, and he asked, 'Do you have somebody especially picked out for me this year?' And I said, 'You know what, Isaac? I know exactly who I'm going to give you. I know you had a tough assignment last year, and you did a really good job. I have somebody perfect for you this year. You're going to have to really work with him because he's going to need a lot of encouragement.' And so far, it's worked out great."

need. In this case, you will also choose a buddy who is particularly sensitive and helpful, but you may not need to "prepare" a younger buddy by talking about the situation in advance. Stay close during the first few meetings to make sure that things are OK, and be available to talk with the younger child at any time issues arise.

You may also decide to create a buddy "foursome" to provide extra support for a younger student when his or her older buddy has special needs. In this situation two buddy pairs sit together and are able to work together if they want to or need to. The presence of the other older child can help both children in the special needs pair, by preventing the younger buddy from taking the role of the older buddy, and by providing a relaxed way for the older special needs buddy to interact with an age peer.

One final caution: If you match special needs students with particularly caring, thoughtful, and mature buddies, these children may be pleased with the challenge, but they may also feel uncomfortable about being singled out. Your matching decisions and whether to bring students into the decision rely above all on your best judgment.

When Pairs Despair

If problems arise with particular buddy pairs, it's always advisable to try to help the students learn to resolve their conflicts. After some time, however, you may decide that it's better to put your effort elsewhere and, in this case, switch the buddies. Make sure that the buddies you switch with are willing and able, and that you do not disrupt a compatible, happy pair. Some teachers say that they never switch a buddy pair, primarily because they see any given relationship as an opportunity for students to learn to work things out.

Beyond Initial Planning

While your initial planning has been the focus here, you'll also want to get together with your partner after every Buddies meeting to reflect and plan for your next meeting. You may each want to designate a small notebook or journal as the place to keep your reflections about how to change or improve an activity. You can use the same journal for making your observation notes during the buddy activities.

It's also nice to be able to share ideas and experiences at grade-level or schoolwide staff meetings. Some schools set aside time during monthly grade-level meetings to talk about Buddies, and others set aside some in-service time to meet and talk about Buddies.

Checking in to share observations about buddy pairs and buddy activities is an essential ingredient in a successful Buddies program. ▼

PART 3

Making It Work
with Students

You've met with your partner, decided how often your two classes will meet, planned some initial getting-to-know-each-other activities, and agreed how to "buddy up" the students. That's a lot of groundwork behind you! At last it's time to introduce your students to the goals for your Buddies program and to help them prepare for their first meeting and the year ahead.

Preparing the Students

How you introduce the Buddies program to your students makes a difference. If you want students to be caring and thoughtful of their buddies, show them that these goals are important to you – by making the time to discuss them and by helping students anticipate what it will mean to be a buddy.

Introducing the Idea of Buddies to Older Students

You may want to introduce Buddies to the older students by explaining that they will have the opportunity to be a buddy or an "older friend" to a younger child, to help the younger child, and to be a caring role model. Often teachers take a few minutes to tell a story about a time when they were younger and had a special "older friend" and then ask students to talk about their own experiences. Do they have any older friends that they look up to? What do they like about having older friends? If students have been younger buddies themselves, invite them to talk about how that felt and what they learned from it.

You may also want to ask if any of the students already know some younger child well – a friend, a younger sibling, a neighbor, a cousin? Invite students to share with the class what it's like to be an older friend to a younger person. What do they like about it? Are there times they don't like it? Why?

" We took the time to incorporate talking about patience and caring and the ways you can question, and all that, trying to make Buddies a meaty kind of learning and real, true relationship building."

"Patience is really important. It's one of those things that you either get, or else you have a hard time getting along with others. What I like about Buddies is that it gives children the opportunity to develop patience at an early age."

....

Ask children to imagine some of the difficulties that may arise as they work with younger children. What are some possible solutions? For example, what ideas do the children have about what to do if their younger buddy is very shy? What are some different things they might try? Ask children to imagine some of the worries the younger children might have. What could they do to help the younger ones feel more comfortable? What kinds of things might they want to avoid?

By having a chance to talk about these issues in advance, students will be prepared to respond more positively and helpfully to their younger buddies. And they will also be learning that positive relationships with others don't happen by chance; they happen best when we bring to them a thoughtful, caring, problem-solving approach.

Introducing the Idea of Buddies to Younger Students

When preparing very young children for a Buddies program, remember that some of them will have no idea what a "buddy" is. Explain in detail how the children will meet their buddies, how these older children are going to help them, and some of the ways the older buddies will have fun with them.

You may choose to begin a discussion by asking whether any of the children have an older friend or sibling and what they like about spending time with someone older. Ask them what is hard sometimes about spending time with someone older. Allow plenty of time for children to discuss their worries and ask questions. Kindergartners especially can be frightened of all those "big kids" and need time to talk about their fears and feelings.

Introducing Buddy Partners for the Very First Time

Students most likely will be excited to meet their buddies, but they may feel nervous and awkward with one another at first. That's why it's helpful to make the introduction and first activity as comfortable, nonthreatening, and enjoyable as possible.

The First Day

Talk with your partner in advance and plan exactly how you will introduce the children for the first time. What matters most is that the introductions feel warm and caring — that students don't feel that their name is just being read off a list. One successful approach is to have older children seated and quiet as their younger buddies come into the room. If you ask the younger children their names (one at a time), you can then say, "Oh, your older buddy is

Big kids can be scary to little kids on the first day of Buddies — but they're shorter and less intimidating if they're seated! ▼

going to be (name of child)," and have the older child come up and meet the younger buddy. The two can then sit down together. Some teachers divide the classes in half and work out of two rooms to help children feel less overwhelmed for this first meeting. Another way to help children feel comfortable is to have them send each other a note or drawing introducing themselves and welcoming the other to their "buddyship" before their first meeting.

Letting Parents Know

Let parents and other caretaking adults know that you have a Buddies program at your school or in your classroom. In a brief note home, describe some of the benefits for both older and younger children (see the "Sample Letter Home" on page 136 in the Resources section).

After children meet with their buddies for the first time, have them prepare a buddy "introduction" for their parents or another adult at home (in most cases these will be reports, not actual meetings). The introductions might be anchored by something the buddies created together, such as buddy portraits or a record of their buddy interviews. Have students practice with their buddies how they will introduce each other at home. (See the activity "Bringing Buddy Home" on page 70.)

Before Each Activity

You will find that all of the activities suggested in Part 4 involve "introductory" classroom work to prepare both older and younger children for what they will do during Buddies time. For each activity, we encourage you to help children practice and prepare for what they will be doing during Buddies time. For example, in the first activity – "Buddy Interview" – older students brainstorm ideas about how to share personal information with their younger buddies and then practice the interviewing process on each other. Younger students, too, discuss in advance what they would like to know about their buddies and what they would like to share about themselves, and then practice the asking and telling by interviewing their classmates.

You may also decide to incorporate "b-mail" into your Buddies program. This simply means giving children a chance to send each other a note or invitation anticipating their upcoming buddy time together (see a description of b-mail on page 42).

Student Reflection Time

Because reflection is so integral to learning, you will want to provide children with regular ways to reflect on their buddy experiences. Consider mixing reflection structures that involve discussion, writing, and drawing, and that involve the buddy classes together and apart. (See the "Class Reflection Guide" on page 138 in the Resources section.)

Many of the activities described in Part 4 suggest that buddies make a record of their activity, either as part of the activity or in a journal (for more information about buddy journals, see page 42). When buddies have done this and you keep the two classes together to reflect, begin by inviting volunteers to describe what they wrote or drew. Follow up with questions about what the buddies learned about working with each other. If children describe problems they encountered working with their buddies, keep the discussion focused on problem solving, not blaming; that way everyone can see that it's normal to have problems and it's normal to try to solve them.

Sometimes you may conclude the activity by asking the gathered buddy pairs a simple open-ended question such as "How'd it go today?" Be prepared to

> 66 *At the end of all the buddy activities I have a debriefing in the sense of, 'How did it go, what would you do differently, how are things working out?' It puts you in touch with what the kids are dealing with and it gives other students a chance to hear similar problems or even chime in their two cents. I find debriefing is very important. It moves us to other levels.*

help students recognize what they learned, what they enjoyed, and what they want to improve.

There will be times when you choose to save reflection about the buddy experience until each class is back in its own classroom. These "private" reflection times can be especially useful for the older buddies. Their greater responsibility for the success of the buddy relationship and their longer attention span for discussion and problem solving can make these after-the-fact sessions a time for real growth. In addition, by providing structured time to hear from the children (and to share your own observations), you build openness in your own classroom and give students practice helping each other address challenges.

For the younger buddies, private reflection time is an opportunity to bring up concerns that they may feel uncomfortable talking about in front of their older buddy. But don't let it become a time monopolized by problems and worries. Be sure children also have a chance to talk about what they enjoy about Buddies and what they are learning.

The Ongoing Cycle of Preparation and Reflection

An essential aspect of Buddies is the cycle we have just described: preparation time with the students before every activity and reflection time with them afterwards. Of course, the length and content of the preparation and reflection will vary depending on the activity.

In general, it's useful for students to have some time before each activity to learn about what they will be doing with their buddies, brainstorm ways to have a successful session, and practice the activity in their own classroom, if necessary. Even if students are already familiar with their buddies and with the

66 *You have to take time to do that unity building. You can't just say, 'Go out and share and care for each other.' You have to show them how it's done."*

◀ At the end of a Buddies activity, children consolidate their academic and social learning by talking about how it went and what they learned.

activities they will be carrying out, it is still important to take a few minutes beforehand to have students bring to mind any goals or directions they may have set for themselves after their last meeting.

As with preparation, reflection will sometimes be very brief and sometimes more involved, depending upon what students bring up. Even when things are going very well, we encourage you to take a few minutes to let the children themselves acknowledge what went well, what they enjoyed, and what they are learning. You could also use this time to invite children to share ideas about what they would like to do with their buddies in the future.

❝ The kids love coming up with their own ideas about how to spend time with their buddies. We've learned to go with their initiative and enthusiasm."

Two Routines That Add Motivation and Meaning

One of the pleasures of a Buddies program is the regularity and structure it gives to forming relationships; another is the surprise it can interject. Buddy mail (or b-mail) and buddy journals are two ways to build both structure and surprise into your program and to add motivation and meaning to the buddy experience.

"Parents have told me that their children treasure these letters."

b-mail

Some of the buddy activities you decide on will clearly lend themselves to an invitation from the buddies in one class to their buddies in the other. For example, the older buddies may decide to host the younger children on a trip to the zoo. Or the younger children may want to prepare a Valentine party for their older buddies. A decorated invitation adds importance and pleasure to the event for both the child making the invitation and the child receiving it. (B-mail is also a good way to practice saying "thank you" when an event is over and there are memories to share.)

But not all b-mail needs to be elaborate or tied to a special event. You could choose to make b-mail a regular language arts activity and a purposeful way to foster buddies' communication with one another. For example, buddies who will be interviewing each other about a favorite book can send each other hints about the book they plan to share. Buddies who will be going on a neighborhood walk together can write or draw about what they hope to see. Buddies can also write or draw about personal news, such as a visiting aunt, a broken bicycle, or a new kitten.

Have children send buddy mail before every meeting, or to announce occasional special events, or whenever the spirit strikes. The only rule is that every buddy in the receiving class *must* get mail. This means that if students are absent, you or other students must be substitute correspondents, or else you can hold up the delivery until any absent students return and add their mail to the rest. If you're going to build b-mail into your program, it's also fun to have specially decorated mailboxes in each room.

Buddy Journals or Portfolios

Buddy journals or portfolios are valuable as a way to have students compile a "historical" record of their time together. Some teachers designate the journals

Dear Buddies,
Could you please come to our classroom. We love you. We like you buddies. We wish you come to the carnival with us. Buddies we wish you could come to our, everyday ♡!
room
Hugs and kisses

as the place for buddies to record any writing, drawing, or problem solving they do as part of a given activity, as well as any conclusions or reflections buddies have about the activity and their time together. Portfolios can serve the same purpose, as a place to collect buddy products and buddy reflections. These collections are a concrete way for the buddies to see how much they are accomplishing together and to remember their favorite times. (See also the activity "Starting Buddy Journals" on page 58.)

If you and your buddy teacher decide to have the children keep journals, decide also whether the pairs will keep one journal together or two separate journals. There are advantages and disadvantages to both alternatives.

Shared Journals. A shared journal reinforces the shared nature of the relationship and gives the buddies a common prized possession. Its drawbacks include the ease with which recording in it may be

▲ *B-mail can be from the whole class, or each student can write a personal note — either way, it's always appreciated.*

66 *Every time the buddies finish an activity, they write it into their journals. They enjoy that."*

▲ *Buddy journals and portfolios are a convenient way for buddies to collect their thoughts and store their work.*

appropriated by the older buddy, and the dilemma of how to share it at the end of the year. One approach that mitigates both problems is to create looseleaf journals with large enough paper that the buddies have space enough to work simultaneously. At the end of the year, you can photocopy the pages and have buddies reconstitute their journal into two journals, each with alternating original and photocopied pages.

Individual Journals. If you choose to have buddies keep individual journals, the children are less constrained by each other's need for space or access to a particular portion of the page. They also are able to keep all of their original work, an advantage if much of it has colorful decorations or drawings. The disadvantage, of course, is that each child ends up with a record of only his or her half of the buddy experience.

Hints from Teachers and Troubleshooting Suggestions

Many of the teachers interviewed for this book have been doing Buddies for years. The hints and suggestions below come from some of their tried-and-true successes and some of their worst nightmares.

- **Food Is Fun.** To help buddies build positive feelings toward each other, provide them with positive associations: Feed them! The simplest snack can be a festive occasion in the middle of the school day. Socializing around food is fun!

- **Take a Walk.** Another way to make Buddies special is to get the children out of the building. Take a walk with them. The walk can have a particular destination (such as the ice cream store) or a particular purpose (such as a nature walk). The teacher of the younger buddies will especially enjoy having personal shoelace helpers.

- **Provide Pairs with a Concrete Focus.** Some buddies may be more comfortable together when they have a concrete problem to solve or a concrete object to discuss. Games with math manipulatives or interviews about a favorite book or special object take some of the pressure off the buddies to be captivating all on their own.

- **Make a Schedule and Stick to It.** Children look forward to their Buddies time. Try to make it a regular time once a week, and don't consider it "soft" time that can be bumped at will. Young buddies have been known to cry when their Buddies time is disrupted.

- **Be Spontaneous (Even Though You've Got a Schedule and Stick to It).** Don't be afraid occasionally to honor children's needs to be spontaneous. A quick interruption of the spelling test for a spontaneous buddy "thank you" will probably be forgiven!

" When our buddy classes decided to raise money for a teacher whose classroom had been destroyed by a fire, we looked to the children to lead the way. Within no time they started a schoolwide recycling drive and advertised with posters, letters to teachers, and visits to other classrooms to promote the idea. For two months they kept working on it, and they raised almost $200! When they set their own goal and saw that they could accomplish their goal, it gave them so much joy."

Whether it's a special ▶
excursion or a routine class
activity, there's probably
a natural way to invite
buddies to join in.

" *It's wonderful to see the*
kids holding hands again."

....

- **Look for Natural Ways to Include Buddies.**
  Once your antennae are out, you'll find lots of
  ways to make a one-class project into a Buddies
  project. Are your kids collecting leaves for a
  report? Have them invite their buddies along. Are
  they rehearsing a skit for Open House? Those
  buddies make an appreciative audience. Are they
  doing science experiments, lunch patrol, or bulletin boards? You know who to call.

- **Ours Is Best!** Whoops. Don't put buddy pairs
  into a situation that they can easily turn into a
  competition or contest. This goes for activities
  within the classroom and for schoolwide activities
  that all the buddy classes may participate in.

- **Final Product: Friend or Foe?** Sometimes a
  final product helps buddies focus – or is even the
  point of the activity. But sometimes a final product introduces a level of competitiveness or performance stress that is harmful to the buddy
  relationship.

- **Stranded!** No matter how much your children
  love Buddies, you will always have absences on
  Buddies day. You will also have children who are
  absent for long periods or who move away, leav-

ing their buddy "stranded." Accordingly, some teachers ask for volunteers who will create a "buddy threesome" – for the day, until the buddy returns to school, for the rest of the year, or until there is a new buddy match. Others prefer to have all buddy pairs also paired loosely into "buddy foursomes," as described below.

- **Foursomes.** There is a lot to be said for creating buddy foursomes (two sets of buddies). The foursomes do not supercede the pair relationships, but they sit near each other and can help out. Although they interact only informally, they can provide an instant "home" for children whose buddies are absent or move away, or extra support for pairs in which one of the children has special needs.

- **Midyear Goodbyes.** There are many sad stories of children who suddenly moved away in the middle of the year and didn't get a chance to say goodbye to their buddy. This can be hard on both children. Be vigilant in communicating to your buddy teacher as soon as you know one of the children in your class will be moving away. Make a special way, if possible, for the buddies to say goodbye.

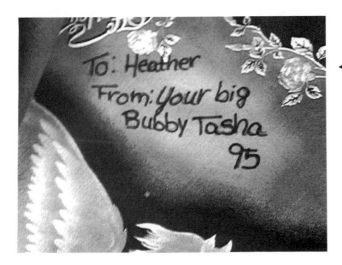

◀ *Sometimes buddies who move away or graduate to middle school like to leave a farewell memento with their buddies.*

It's always an adventure to ▶
go on a field trip — especially
when buddies are invited
along.

● **Lost at the Zoo.** Just because you expect older
buddies to be responsible for their younger
buddy on a field trip, it doesn't always happen. It
may help if everybody agrees to hold hands and
to keep track of another pair of buddies (those
foursomes, again), but even mothers have been
known to lose track of six-year-olds. As part of
planning with your classes for the field trip, have
children suggest ways they can make sure they
stay together and what they can do if they get
separated. One teacher shares this story of a
Buddies day at the zoo that turned out to be just
that — "zoo-y."

> "Our buddy classes went on a field trip
> together, and I simply overestimated my kids'
> abilities to really watch their younger buddies
> — they are just kids themselves. Some of the
> older kids got separated from the rest of us —
> they were lost and they had a few of the
> younger buddies with them. It worked out
> because the older kids sought help from the
> zoo staff, but that wasn't the end of it. Even
> after we were all together again, my partner
> and I were very upset. All day we kept finding

kids without their buddies. And each time it happened, I got more frantic. By the end of the day I was screeching at everyone, 'Where is your buddy! Where is your buddy!'

"We talked about it the next day, both with the students and then just the two of us. We hadn't been clear about our expectations – with each other or with the kids. We shared ideas about how we might do it differently in the future. It was important to communicate, express our disappointment, and make sure that we were still OK with each other."

This zoo story is important, not to scare you off Buddies, but to let you know that even experienced buddy classes can have disasters and recover – as long as everyone communicates about what happened.

PART 4

Activity Ideas

- Getting to Know You
- Learning Together
- Stepping Out
- Celebrating Our Year

GETTING TO KNOW YOU

THE BEGINNING of Buddies is an important time as it sets the tone for the whole year. You will want children to see right from the start that building relationships is a main focus of Buddies, and that they will have plenty of opportunities to get to know and learn about each other throughout the year.

The getting-to-know-you activities that follow involve students in talking, thinking, writing, drawing, and reading together as they share experiences and get to know each other. At the same time that buddy friendships begin to form, buddy classes will be developing habits of preparing for their meetings together and reflecting thoughtfully upon the experience afterwards.

- **Buddy Interview**
- **Starting Buddy Journals**
- **Buddy Portrait**
- **Question Game**
- **Bringing Buddy Home**

Buddy Interview

Buddy Interview is a very flexible structure for use both early on and throughout the year. It typically takes the form of buddies interviewing each other about an object each has brought to share, such as a favorite book, or about a topic of personal interest to each buddy, such as something each child is proud to be able to do. Then each partner (or the pair together) records in words and/or pictures something that was learned about the buddy during the interview.

At the beginning of the year, Buddy Interview is an especially useful, low-key way to have buddies get to know each other and share information about themselves. For a first buddy interview, try Talking Artifacts (see below), which is structured by having children ask each other questions about a special object brought from home. Interviews such as Talking Artifacts that have a concrete focus make it easy for the buddies to get started. The artifacts' concrete presence also helps children think of connections to new questions and more elaborated answers.

Activity Structure

In their separate classrooms, older and younger students brainstorm a list of possible questions to ask their buddies. During Buddies time, buddies interview each other, practice answering expansively and using follow-up questions, and then record in words and/or pictures some of what they learn about each other. To conclude the activity, students reflect on what they enjoyed about working with their buddies and what they learned from the experience.

Planning with Your Buddy Teacher

Pick a topic that will be unthreatening and inclusive for all students. Imagine your children going through the interview process: What will help them succeed? What are potential pitfalls? Will a final product be a help or a hindrance? With your partner, review the steps described below, making adjustments as needed.

Introducing the Activity with Older Students

- **Is this the first buddy activity of the year?** If this is the first Buddies activity of the year, begin by having a discussion about what it means to be an older buddy, what might be challenging about working with a younger buddy, and any other questions or concerns that students may have. For more specific suggestions, see "Preparing the Students," page 35.

- **Describe the purpose of the interview.** Introduce the interview topic. Explain that the most important thing about the interview is for buddies to enjoy finding out new things about each other. In addition, have children discuss some of the benefits of learning how to conduct interviews and be interviewed.

- **Model the interview.** If your students are unfamiliar with partner interviewing, model a buddy interview with a volunteer from the class. Demonstrate wait time and open-ended questioning, and show them how to elaborate answers and make connections to new ideas.

  If your students are already familiar with partner interviewing, help them see how buddy interviews will be similar to the interviews they do with classmates and how they will be different.

- **Have students brainstorm interview questions.** Ask students what questions related to the interview topic they could ask their younger buddies and what questions they would like to answer. Create a list of students' question ideas on the board for them to consider. You might also have students choose a few and write them down for reference during their interview.

- **Let students practice the interview process on their classmates.** Have older students practice the interview process on each other (this is a good way for classmates to get to know each other, as well as their buddies!). Consider posting a list of open-ended follow-up prompts (see examples under "Materials," below).

- **Discuss the challenges of working with younger buddies.** Lead a discussion about how students can make this activity successful with their younger buddies. Help students anticipate possible rough spots: What can you do if your buddy is very shy? What can you do if your buddy is having a hard time asking questions? Invite children to think about what they will do to help their younger buddies feel cared for and special.

Introducing the Activity with Younger Students

- **Is this the first buddy activity of the year?** If this is the first Buddies activity of the year, tell the children about their buddy class and some of the things they will be doing together. Ask students what they are looking forward to about Buddies and what they may be worried about. Invite the children to talk about their experiences having or being older siblings, and discuss with them how buddies and siblings may be alike and different.

- **Describe the purpose of the interview.** Introduce the interview topic. Explain that the most important thing about the interview is for buddies to enjoy finding out new things about each other.

- **Model the interview.** Model a buddy interview about the topic by having a student or aide ask you a few questions (you may choose to provide these).

- **Have students brainstorm interview questions.** Ask students what questions they would like to ask their older buddies to get to know them better, and what kinds of things they would like to tell their buddies about themselves.

- **Let children practice the interview process on their classmates.** Have children practice this type of partner interview with each other (these interviews are a great way to build a sense of community within your classroom). A bit of practice can be reassuring for the children and should contribute to the success of their buddy interviews.

b-mail

Have buddies send each other a note or postcard anticipating the interview and getting together.

Doing the Activity

- **Is this the first buddy activity of the year?** If this is the first time buddies are meeting each other, take a few minutes to introduce the children to their buddies (see "Introducing Buddy Partners for the Very First Time," page 37).

- **Circulate and observe.** Once the children are paired off and working together, circulate and observe the buddy pairs. Be aware of the students who are quietly ignoring each other as well as the ones who may be wrangling or making noise. You may want to pay particular attention to children who are very shy, who have trouble attending, or who have special needs.

- **Make notes.** Make notes in your journal for use in reflecting with the students at the conclusion of the activity and for reflecting later with your buddy teacher.

- **Provide options for buddies who finish early.** Students who finish the activity early can find another pair who are finished and take turns telling each other what they learned about their buddy (with permission from the buddy, of course).

- **Have buddies discuss their experience.** Invite children to discuss what went well and what they enjoyed. It's also important for students to have the opportunity to discuss any difficulties they may have had. Ask children what challenges or rough spots they encountered and what they learned as a result.

Buddy Journals

If you have already introduced buddy journals (see the activity "Starting Buddy Journals" on page 58), have students record something about their time together. Older buddies can write while younger buddies draw, or the buddies can combine forces with a language-experience approach (the younger buddy dictates and the older buddy records).

Reflecting

With your separate classes, have students talk about what they are learning about being buddies and what is hard.

With your buddy teacher, discuss afterwards what went well and what was challenging. Refer to any observation notes you made and add to them any information that will help you (or a colleague seeking advice) repeat or adapt the activity. Discuss any observations you or your partner made about individual buddy pairs and what interventions, if any, might be called for in the future.

Interview Topics

■ **Talking Artifacts.** Buddies each bring in a prized "artifact," something that has special meaning for them, such as a letter from a grandparent, a ticket stub from a baseball game, a favorite birthday present, something they made for their mother when they were "little," etc. It is a good idea to have children bring their artifacts in a paper bag or other container that will keep them concealed (and out of "play") until the interview begins.

■ **Favorite Books.** Buddies each bring a favorite book from home or the school or class library collection to share. They present their book (by reading it, describing it, acting out a favorite scene, etc.) and their buddy interviews them about it.

■ **I Can.** Buddies each think of something they like to do or are proud to be able to do, such as counting by fives, making their bed, rollerblading, keeping a fish tank, etc. Buddies ask each other about the special thing the other "can do" and make a drawing that shows the partner doing the special thing. Captions or short narratives can accompany the drawings.

■ **Helping Hands.** Buddies interview each other about a way each of them helps at home or at school, or about a particular time each of them helped someone. They then trace each other's hand and draw the partner's story inside the outline of his or her hand. Captions or short narratives can accompany the drawings.

■ **I Wonder.** Buddies each think of a topic or big question they wonder about, such as "Do fish sleep?" or "Why is there war?" Buddies interview each other about how they got their "wonder" and discuss it with them.

■ **Buddy Facts.** Buddies compile a list of or make drawings that illustrate simple facts about each other, such as birth date, number of brothers and sisters, favorite food, worst food, and pets or favorite animals.

■ **Alike and Different.** Buddies compare the facts they learn about each other by charting them in a Venn Diagram.

■ **Portfolio Sharing.** Buddies interview each other about something each has selected from his or her classroom portfolio (see the full activity description on page 100).

■ **Bringing Buddy Home.** Buddies help each other prepare for an at-home interview in which they tell a parent or other caregiver about their buddy and what they do together (see the full activity description on page 70).

Materials

- Any artifacts, books, or other concrete objects used in the interview
- Older buddies' lists of interview questions (optional)
- List of follow-up prompts (optional):

    I wonder . . .
    What else . . .
    Why was that important to you?
    Tell me more . . .
    Go on . . .
    Give me a little more detail . . .
    Hmmm . . .
    So . . .
    I can't quite picture that . . .
    Why did you tell me that?
    What do you think you learned from doing this?
    How do you feel about doing this?
    What do you still wonder about?

Starting Buddy Journals

Since many buddy activities involve the buddies in writing and drawing together, and since for every buddy activity you will be asking buddies to reflect on how they're doing, why not have them create a special place to collect their work and their thoughts—in either joint or individual journals?

When you introduce the idea of buddy journals, you help students visualize a yearlong relationship with their buddy. They can begin to imagine the things they will do together and the words and pictures that will accumulate in their journals. When buddies spend time making the journal covers or booklets to use as journals, they begin the process of committing themselves to a new responsibility and a new friendship.

Activity Structure

In their separate classrooms, students discuss the purpose of keeping a journal and what keeping a buddy journal might be like. When the buddies come together, they make journal covers or booklets. To conclude, the students talk about what they did and how it went. They then draw and/or write their first entries.

Planning with Your Buddy Teacher

Do the older students have experience keeping journals? If many of them are unfamiliar with journals, you may wish to delay this activity until they have begun keeping journals for math, reading, or some other purpose. The older students should be able to help their younger buddies understand the use of journals for reflecting as well as recording.

Make some decisions together about the buddy journals: Will buddies keep portfolios, journals, or both? Will they keep them individually or jointly? (See the descriptions of various journal formats at the end of this activity.) Will the journals be part of every buddy activity or will you alternate them with other kinds of reflection? How will you want to distribute the recorded reflections and products of the buddy pairs at the end of the year?

After making such decisions, review the steps described below (they describe joint, looseleaf journals). Make adjustments depending on the journal or portfolio format your classes will be using.

Introducing the Activity with Older Students

- **Discuss the purpose and challenge of keeping joint journals.** Have students discuss the benefits and burdens of keeping journals with their buddies. What will the journals add to their buddy experience? What are some specific challenges the older buddies will face? Have them talk about ways to encourage and help their buddies without taking over. Have them talk about when they might need extra patience.

- **Discuss the cover-making activity.** Have students talk about what they want the cover for their joint journal to represent. How can they get their younger buddies to talk about what's important to them? How can they share responsibility for the ideas and work of making the cover? How can they be sure their buddy feels included?

Introducing the Activity with Younger Students

- **Show students some sample journals.** Describe some of the activities and feelings that children have written and drawn about in the samples.

- **Describe the purpose of keeping buddy journals.** Tell children about some of the experiences they will write and draw about with their buddies. Talk with them about why it will be nice to have a record of those times.

- **Discuss the cover-making activity.** Have students talk about what they want the cover for their joint journal to represent. How can they talk with their buddies about their ideas? How can they make sure they do their part in making the cover?

b-mail

Have buddies send each other ideas for a title for their journal.

Doing the Activity

- **Review the journal purpose and the goals of the cover-making activity.** With both classes together, have students review the purpose of the journal and the challenges involved in helping their buddy and doing their own part of the cover.

- **Observe, make notes, respond to students.** While students are working, circulate among the pairs. Help students reflect on the activity goals, if necessary. Think about possible topics for later discussion with the students and make a note of any issues you will want to bring up later with your buddy teacher.

- **Have buddies reflect on their experience.** Invite children to talk about how it went. What was fun? What was hard? What did they learn? What are they looking forward to about keeping a journal? What are they looking forward to about having a buddy?

Buddy Journals

Have buddies make their first journal entry. As a group have students brainstorm a list of things they thought or felt or did as part of working with their buddy and making the cover. Then have the buddies choose from the list something to write or draw about. Buddy pairs may choose to collaborate on a single entry or to make separate, side-by-side entries.

Reflecting

With your separate classes, have students talk about what they are learning about being buddies and what is hard.

With your buddy teacher, discuss afterwards what went well and what was challenging. Discuss any observations you or your partner made about individual buddy pairs and what interventions, if any, might be called for in the future.

Journal Variations

■ **Joint Journals.** A shared journal gives students a concrete representation of their partnership. If it is constructed out of large sheets of paper (11″ × 17″), it will be easier for the buddies to work in it simultaneously. If it is loosely bound (or bound with center staples that can be removed), it will be easier to disassemble at the end of the year to make photocopies of the pages for reassembly into two complete journals. In this case, have buddies alternate original and photocopied pages in the reconstituted journals and make a new cover for the second journal.

■ **Joint Portfolio.** Portfolios have the advantage of flexibility – products of any size can be saved in them. The journals themselves can be one product in the portfolio.

■ **Individual Journals.** Students are neither constrained nor overwhelmed by their buddy if each has a separate journal. And they are still free to be guest authors or illustrators in each other's journal.

■ **Individual Bound Journals.** Although pages can't be added to or removed from them, bound books lend importance to buddy time and the buddy relationships. Such books work best as individual journals, since they can't be easily disassembled at the end of the year.

Materials

- Supplies for making journals or portfolios
- Art supplies for making or decorating covers
- Sample journals to show younger students

Buddy Portrait

Buddy Portrait is a creative and concrete way for buddies to picture themselves as a pair. As they draw themselves holding hands or in a scene doing something together, children can be consciously or unconsciously exploring ideas about what it will mean for them to be partners.

The portraits can become part of a large collage of all the cutout buddy portraits, or they can be an early entry in the buddy journals.

Activity Structure

In their separate classrooms, older and younger students think ahead about what it may be like to work with their buddies on this activity. Together buddies create their collage or journal portraits. To conclude the activity, students reflect on what they enjoyed about being with their buddies and what they learned from the process.

Planning with Your Buddy Teacher

Decide whether to do a collage or journal activity. If you decide to do a collage, decide how the collage background will be made. Will it be plain? Will one buddy class make it? Will the buddy classes do it together (see "Scenic Collage" on page 64)? With your partner, review the steps described below, making adjustments as needed.

Introducing the Activity with Older Students

- **Describe the activity and ask for students' ideas.** Ask students why it might be fun or valuable to make buddy portraits. Have students brainstorm scenes in which the buddies could be pictured for a journal entry, or ideas about what kinds of buddy cutouts could go on the collage. (If you are making a collage, explain that each buddy pair will cut out its twosome drawing or painting and glue it onto the collage.)

- **Discuss potential challenges of the activity.** What can the older buddies do to share the drawing or painting? How can they keep their younger buddies engaged? How can they make the activity fun?

Introducing the Activity with Younger Students

- **Describe the activity and ask for students' ideas.** Describe the collage or journal activity. Have students brainstorm scenes in which the buddies could be pictured, or ideas about what kinds of buddy cutouts could go on the collage. (If you are making a collage, explain that each buddy pair will cut out its twosome drawing or painting and glue it onto the collage.)

- **Discuss potential challenges of the activity.** Ask students to think about how they can do their part of the drawing or painting. How can they help their buddy? What can they do to make the activity fun?

b-mail

Have older buddies send their younger buddies an invitation to have their portrait made.

Doing the Activity

- **Ask pairs to decide how to share the work.** Remind them of variations in how they can do this: each draw the other, each draw oneself, or both draw both. If buddies will be adding their cutouts to a collage, have them think about how the two of them will decide where to attach their cutout.

- **Observe.** Once students are working, observe the buddy pairs. If necessary, ask pairs how they are sharing the work or how to make their illustration work as a cutout for the collage.

- **Make notes for future reflection.** As buddies work together, make notes in your buddy journal for use in reflecting with the students and for reflecting later with your buddy teacher.

- **Have buddies discuss their experience.** Invite children to discuss what they enjoyed about making portraits and what they learned about each other. Give students the opportunity to discuss any difficulties they may have had. Ask children what challenges or rough spots they encountered and what they learned as a result.

Buddy Journals

If the portraits become part of a collage instead of entries in the buddy journals, have students write or draw in their journals about working together on the collage.

Reflecting

With your separate classes, have students talk about what they are learning about being buddies and what is hard.

With your buddy teacher discuss afterwards what went well and what was challenging. Refer to any observation notes you made and add to them any information that will help you (or a colleague seeking advice) repeat or adapt the activity. Discuss any observations you or your partner made about individual buddy pairs.

Portrait Variations

■ **Scenic Collage.** For this two-part activity, buddy pairs first contribute to a background for the collage, and then make their buddy portraits for mounting on the background.

■ **Factoid Buddies.** Buddies draw outline portraits of each other that they fill with facts and drawings about each other and what they do together.

■ **Photographically Us.** Buddy pairs are photographed in poses they have devised. Then they write the story of their photo to accompany it as an entry in their journals, for a page in a whole-group buddies' book, or as part of a bulletin board display.

Materials

● Drawing, painting, or collage materials for buddy pairs

● Butcher paper for collage background, glue (optional)

● Camera (Photographically Us)

Question Game

Question Game lets buddies tell each other about themselves in a game format that children love. Elements of chance and turn-taking spice up a set of questions about likes and dislikes and hopes and fears—questions that are open-ended so that children can elaborate to whatever degree they feel comfortable.

Question Game can be played early in the year to help students get to know each other or later in the year when they feel relaxed and expansive. The questions can be those provided, those the students invent, or both.

Activity Structure

One or both classes practice the game so that at least one member of each buddy pair knows how to play. During Buddies time, buddy pairs play the game together. Buddies take turns picking a question out of a bag and giving it to their buddy to ask them. They may also write new questions to extend the game. To conclude the activity, students reflect on what they enjoyed about their time together, what was hard, and what they learned about each other and being a buddy.

Planning with Your Buddy Teacher

Decide whether both classes will practice the game before coming together for Buddies time, or whether one class will host the game and teach it to their buddies. Review the provided questions, adding or deleting questions as appropriate for your classes. Then make a master sheet of questions and duplicate them for the buddy pairs; leave some blank spaces where students can write their own questions, if you wish.

Introducing the Activity with Older Students

- **Do or do not introduce the game.** If the older students are hosting the game, or if neither class is hosting the game, introduce it to your students. Show them the sheet of questions and an already assembled bag of playing cards.

  If the younger students are hosting the game, they will teach it to their buddies. Simply let your students know they will be playing a question game with their buddies.

- **Do a demonstration.** With a volunteer, demonstrate playing the game. Pick a card at random out of the bag and hand it to your partner. Your partner reads the question aloud, and you answer it. Trade roles and have your partner pick a question and hand it to you. Read the question aloud; when your partner answers it, model asking follow-up questions. If appropriate, model adding new questions: with your partner, make up a question of your own, write it on a blank question card, and add it to the bag.

- **Have partners try the game.** Distribute a small bag, scissors, and a copy of the sheet of questions to each pair of students. Partners cut up the questions, put them in the bag, give it a shake, and get started.

- **Discuss playing the game with buddies.** Invite students' ideas about playing this game with their younger buddies. How can they change the game if their buddy can't read? What can they do if their buddy is very shy? What if there is a question the buddy doesn't understand? What if there is a question the buddy doesn't want to answer?

Introducing the Activity with Younger Students

- **Do or do not introduce the game.** If the younger students are hosting the game, or if neither class is hosting the game, introduce it to your students. Show them the sheet of questions and an already assembled bag of playing cards.

  If the older students are hosting the game, they will teach it to their buddies. Simply let your students know they will be playing a question game with their buddies.

- **Do a demonstration.** With a volunteer, demonstrate playing the game. Ask your partner to pick a card at random out of the bag and hand it to you. Read the question out loud for your partner to answer. Model a follow-up question or two. Then you pick a card. If your partner can read, hand the card over; if not, read it aloud yourself and answer the question. Repeat each person's turn. If appropriate, model adding new questions: with your partner, make up a question of your own, write it on a blank question card, and add it to the bag.

- **If your students can read, have partners try the game.** Distribute a small bag, scissors, and a copy of the sheet of questions to each pair of students. Partners cut up the questions, put them in the bag, give it a shake, and get started.

- **Discuss playing the game with buddies.** Ask children to imagine playing this game with their older buddies. What do they hope to learn about their buddy? What do they hope their buddy will learn about them?

b-mail

If either class is hosting the game, have them invite their buddies to play Question Game.

Doing the Activity

- **If necessary, have buddies assemble their bags of question cards.** Most likely, bags will already have been assembled during a practice run in one or both of the classes.

- **Observe, make notes, respond to students.** Once buddies are paired off and working together, circulate and observe. Join various pairs briefly to model asking follow-up questions. If students have blank cards, encourage them to make up their own questions and add them to the bag. Note anything that you might want to reflect on later with students or your buddy teacher.

- **Have buddies reflect on their experience.** Invite children to discuss what they enjoyed about the game and any difficulties they may have had.

Buddy Journals

Have buddies each choose one of their own answers that they want their buddy to write or draw about.

Reflecting

With your separate classes, have students talk about what they are learning about being a buddy and what they are learning about themselves.

With your buddy teacher, discuss afterwards what went well and what was challenging. Refer to any observation notes you made about the activity or about individual buddy pairs.

An Alternative Approach

■ **Custom Questions.** For this variation on the basic game, each buddy class brainstorms their own questions for playing cards. A master sheet of questions from both classes is prepared and copied for buddies to make into playing cards.

Materials

- A sheet of prepared questions, scissors, and a small bag for each classroom "practice" pair or each buddy pair
- Blank master sheet (Custom Questions)

Sample Master Sheet of Questions

What is something that makes you happy?	What is something you would like to do in your life?
What is something you are proud of?	What is something that makes you mad?
What is something that makes you excited?	What is something you like about being a buddy?
What is something you are afraid of?	What is something you hope for?
What is something that hurts your feelings?	What is something you want for the world?
What is something you look forward to?	What is something that makes you sad?
What is something that makes you laugh?	What is something you wish you knew?
What is something you worry about?	

Bringing Buddy Home

Since most buddies won't have a chance to visit each other's homes in person, this interview activity gives students an alternative way to introduce their buddy to parents or other caregivers. The significant adults at home will appreciate learning about this important new friend at school.

In preparation for the at-home interview, children get to imagine themselves being introduced to an important adult in their buddy's life. As a result, the older child's sense of responsibility to the younger buddy may take on new meaning. And at home, as buddies tell an adult about their special friend at school, the adult's interest is bound to add value to the buddy relationship.

Activity Structure

In their separate classrooms, older and younger students brainstorm ideas about what a parent or other adult might enjoy learning about their buddies. Older students will be given a "Buddy Notes" page (see page 74) on which to compile a list of information they already know about their buddy and some information they may still want to find out. Younger students will be given a "Home Activity" page (see pages 75–76) that lists a few questions for a parent or adult to ask about the older buddy. When the buddies get together, the older students find out more about their buddy to write in their notes and then help the younger child go over the questions on the "Home Activity" page. Buddies practice for their home interviews. Students then reflect on their experience working together.

Planning with Your Buddy Teacher

Ideally, children will do Bringing Buddy Home after they have done several other Buddies activities together, some of them getting-to-know-you activities. This way the children will have already accumulated some specific information and experiences to draw on in describing their buddy and their buddy relationship. Also, if parents have already received a letter explaining your overall Buddies program (see "Sample Letter Home," page 136), children will have an easier time introducing their buddies.

With your buddy teacher, plan how the two of you can model successful (and perhaps unsuccessful) ways to get a parent's time and attention for the activity. Plan also to model the classroom practice interviews and the at-home interviews. With your partner, review the steps described below, making adjustments as needed.

We recommend that you invite students to do the activity at home in the home language, so that parents can communicate more easily with their children. We have included a Spanish version of the "Home Activity" page for younger students. If you have parents who speak other languages in your classroom, you may want to have this page translated beforehand. ("Buddy Notes" has not been translated, as older students can use their English page to conduct the activity at home in the home language.)

Introducing the Activity with Older Students

- **Discuss the purpose of introducing buddies at home.** Remind students of the letter you sent home earlier describing the Buddies program in your class. Explain that parents like to hear about who the buddies are and what you do together.

- **Help students anticipate telling about their buddy at home.** Have students brainstorm things a parent or adult might like to know about a buddy and what the buddies do together. Distribute a copy of "Buddy Notes" to each student and have them make notes to themselves under "Things I Know about My Buddy" and "Things I Have to Find Out about My Buddy." Explain that they will have a chance to interview their buddy and make more notes before they take the "Buddy Notes" page home to help them tell someone at home about their buddy.

- **Discuss ways for buddies to practice telling about each other.** Have students think about how to prepare themselves and their younger buddies for talking to someone at home. Show older students the "Home Activity" page their younger buddies will take home; read the questions. Will the younger buddies need to make notes or draw pictures to help them remember? Why will it be important for buddies to listen to what each one plans to tell about the other?

Introducing the Activity with Younger Students

- **Explain the purpose of introducing buddies at home.** Remind students of the letter you sent home earlier describing the Buddies program in your class. Talk about why parents like to hear about who the buddies are and what you do together.

- **Have students brainstorm topics to cover.** Have students begin by talking with a partner about things they could tell a parent or adult about their buddy and what they do together. Then bring the class back together to share their ideas.

- **Show students the "Home Activity" page.** Read the questions aloud and explain that students will practice answering the questions with their older buddy and then will share the "Home Activity" page at home with a parent or other adult. Also, show students the first two sentences of the Home Activity, where they will need to write in their buddies' name and grade. (In the Spanish version, students will also need to circle the appropriate words corresponding to gender.)

b-mail

Have buddies send each other a note identifying someone at home they plan to tell about their buddy.

Doing the Activity

- **Model two buddies preparing for their at-home activity.** With your buddy teacher, one of you take the role of the older buddy and one of you take the role of the younger buddy. Demonstrate going over the questions on the younger child's "Home Activity" page and making notes or drawings. Also model how the older students will check the information on their "Buddy Notes" page and find out more information from their younger buddy. (Use real information about yourselves as you model.)

- **Model what students will do at home.** With your buddy teacher, first model what the "Home Activity" will look like, one of you playing the adult and one the younger buddy. Then model what the "Buddy Notes" activity will look like with an adult and the older buddy.

- **Observe, make notes, respond to students.** As students are working, circulate among the pairs. Encourage children to make notes or draw pictures on the back of their "Home Activity" or "Buddy Notes" page that will help them tell an adult later about their buddy. Note any topics or issues to bring up later for student reflection or to discuss with your buddy teacher.

- **Have buddies reflect on their experience.** Invite children to talk about how it went. What did they learn about each other? What was hard? What are they looking forward to telling someone at home?

Buddy Journals

Have buddies write or draw about something they will tell at home. Perhaps buddies could request a particular entry in each other's journal.

Reflecting

With your separate classes, have students talk about what they are learning about being buddies and what is hard.

With your buddy teacher, discuss afterwards what went well and what was challenging. Decide how to have buddies report back to each other about the at-home interview.

An Alternative Approach

■ **Buddy Interview.** Have buddies take home the product from any buddy interview (see possible interview topics on page 56) as the basis for beginning a conversation with a parent or other adult about their buddy.

Materials

- A "Home Activity" page for each younger student and the teacher of the older students
- A "Buddy Notes" page for each older student

Buddy Notes

Tell your parent or another adult about your younger buddy. Explain what the two of you do together and some of the information you have found out about your buddy. Ask the adult to tell you about a time when he or she had a special childhood friend who was younger (or older).

Things I Know about My Buddy

Things I Have to Find Out about My Buddy

SIGN HERE, PLEASE!

....

....

After you have completed this activity, have everyone who participated sign the sheet and write any comments about the activity on the back. Thank you.

Home Activity

Dear Family Member or Family Friend,

In school this year your child has a special grade ___ "buddy." The buddy's name is _____ . Your child has spent some time in class getting ready to tell you about this special person. Please spend a few minutes talking with your child about his or her buddy.

If you like, you can use the questions below to begin finding out about your child's buddy.

Conversation Starters

■ If your buddy was coming out of school at the end of the day in a big crowd of kids, how would I know which person was your special buddy?

■ If your buddy was on the playground at recess, what would your buddy be doing?

■ If I came into the library, what kind of book would your buddy be reading?

■ If I came into your class at buddy time, what would you and your buddy be doing?

How would your buddy be acting?

How would you be acting?

■ If I asked you what you like best about having a buddy, what would you say?

SIGN HERE, PLEASE!

....

....

After you have completed this activity, each of you please sign your name and the date. If you have any comments about this activity, please write them on the back of this page. Thank you.

Actividad Familiar

Estimados padres, familiares o amigos:

En la escuela, su hijo/su hija tiene un compañero/una compañera especial del _____ grado que se llama _____ . Su hijo o su hija ha estado pensando en algunas cosas que le gustaría compartir con Ud. acerca de esta nueva amistad. Haga el favor de tomar un poco de tiempo para conversar con él o con ella acerca de su nuevo compañero o de su nueva compañera.

Si gusta, puede utilizar las siguientes preguntas para iniciar la conversación.

Para iniciar el diálogo

■ Si, al fin del día, tu compañero o tu compañera estuviera saliendo de la escuela junto con muchos otros niños y niñas, ¿cómo lo reconocería yo a él o a ella?

■ Si tu compañero o tu compañera estuviera en el patio durante el recreo, ¿qué estaría haciendo?

■ Si yo fuera a entrar a la biblioteca, ¿qué libro estaría leyendo tu compañero o tu compañera?

■ Si yo fuera a tu clase a la hora en la cual se reúnen con sus compañeros especiales, ¿qué estarían haciendo tú y tu compañero (o tu y tu compañera)?

> ¿De qué manera se estaría comportando tu compañero o tu compañera?
>
> ¿De qué manera te estarías comportando tú?

■ Si yo te fuera a preguntar qué es lo que más te gusta de tener un compañero especial o una compañera especial, ¿qué me dirías?

¡FIRMEN AQUÍ, POR FAVOR!

....

....

Después de completar esta actividad, haga el favor cada uno de firmar y de escribir la fecha. Si Ud. tiene algún comentario sobre la actividad, por favor escríbalo en el revés de esta hoja. Muchísimas gracias.

LEARNING TOGETHER

BUDDIES ARE always learning together – there's no way around it. But in addition to the overall learning orientation that a Buddies program promotes, you will also find that Buddies can support specific academic goals for both older and younger children. Open-ended learning experiences, teaching or helping experiences, and rehearsal experiences are all ways a Buddies program helps children learn. What they learn can run the gamut – from reading and writing to researching and problem solving to drawing and role-playing.

The activities that follow are designed to be a sampling of what buddies can do together to develop their thinking, to deepen their understandings, to expand their skills, and to enjoy learning with and from each other. You and your students will discover many more as Buddies becomes a natural component of life at school.

- **Reading Together**
- **Character Dialogue**
- **Language Experience**
- **Math Play**
- **Artists Together**
- **Portfolio Sharing**

Reading Together

There's probably no cozier way for buddies to spend time learning, sharing, and enjoying each other's company than by getting their heads together in a book!

While there are many variations of Reading Together, the goal is always to make the experience comfortable, easy, and interesting for both buddies. For example, when buddies read wordless books together, both younger and older students explore making connections and drawing conclusions, and the older students can model ways to elaborate a story narrative. When buddies share their favorite books, both students can practice reading fluently, and in their discussions about the books, the older students can help the younger ones grow as motivated, curious readers.

Activity Structure

In their separate classrooms, partners read lots of stories together (all year long) and spend time sharing the reading, discussing the story ideas, writing and drawing about story connections, and generally experiencing books in a thoughtful and relaxed way. During Buddies time, buddy pairs bring all of these experiences to bear as they curl up with a great book or two. To conclude the activity, students reflect on their shared experience.

Planning with Your Buddy Teacher

Share ideas about ways buddies can enjoy Reading Together activities and help each other become better readers (some specific suggestions are also provided at the end of this activity). Bring each other up to speed on your students' reading experiences: What are students accustomed to? In what ways would you like to help them grow as readers? How can buddy reading be made fun and useful at the same time? Together decide on a particular reading activity for the buddies, then review the steps described below and make adjustments as needed.

Introducing the Activity with Older Students

- **Describe the buddy activity.** Be specific about the activity you have in mind. Describe each buddy's role and some of the reading or language arts goals you have in mind for each student.

- **Have partners practice.** If students will be reading a particular book to their buddies, have them practice reading it to a partner for fluency or expression or drama. Have them think about questions they can ask their buddy that would be interesting to the younger child.

  If students are rusty at any specific aspects of the activity, such as reading wordless books or writing speculative dialogue, have them partner up and practice with a classmate.

- **If the younger buddies will be reading . . .** Talk about how to help younger buddies read without taking over. Have students share their thoughts and ideas about helping their younger buddies become more active readers. Help them see the ways they can involve their younger buddies without taking over.

Introducing the Activity with Younger Students

- **Describe the buddy activity.** Be specific about the activity you have in mind. Describe each buddy's role and some of the reading or language arts goals you have in mind for each student.

- **Model any roles that may be unfamiliar.** If students will be trying something new with their buddies, show them how it will go. Get another adult or a student volunteer to demonstrate with you.

- **Have students practice the activity.** If the activity is one that the students can carry out with a classmate, have them practice.

- **Talk about how students can do their part.** Have students discuss why it will be important for them to do their part.

b-mail

Buddies send each other hints about favorite stories or the book each plans to share.

Doing the Activity

- **Observe, make notes, respond to students.** As you observe the buddy pairs, ask students to describe how they are sharing the reading or the work. Make notes about the activity itself and ways buddies are being successful or unsuccessful at it. Share your observations with students during reflection time or later with your partner.

- **Have buddies discuss their experience.** Invite children to share reflections about what they read and how they felt reading with their buddies. What would they like to repeat or change the next time they read together?

Buddy Journals

Invite students to write or draw about the books they shared.

Reflecting

With your separate classes, have students talk about what they are learning about being a buddy and what they are learning about making reading enjoyable.

With your buddy teacher, share observations about the activity. Is it a good one to repeat? How could it be adapted? Are there particular partnerships that may need more attention?

Reading Together Variations

- **Wordless Books.** Buddies "read" a wordless book together by taking turns telling the story — trading pages, spreads, or other sections of the book. Have students focus on characters' motivation or feelings. Or have them focus on setting the scene. Buddies can also act out dialogue from the story (see "Character Dialogue" on page 82), choose and talk about their favorite illustrations, or speculate about what happens next to the characters.

- **Favorite Picks.** Each child chooses a favorite book to read to or with their buddy. Younger buddies can practice reading to their buddy or can ask their buddy to read a more difficult favorite pick.

- **Shared Reading.** Buddies choose and read a book together, one that the younger buddy can manage. While they read, they share their thoughts and feelings about what's happening in the story. They can also work on a special project, such as a book jacket, an illustration, a dramatization — whatever interests them most.

- **Picture This.** After reading a book together, buddies make a poster to introduce their story to another buddy pair. As a foursome, buddies share their posters with each other and compare their books.

- **Dramarama.** Buddies write a dialogue between two characters they get to know in a story they read together. The dialogue can be driven by the story line or by questions that are on the children's minds: What do you think you will do the next time you want something really badly? What are the pluses and minuses of being the best player on the team? How did you feel about keeping a secret from your sister?

Materials

- Books!
- Drawing and writing supplies

Character Dialogue

Character Dialogue is a creative way for buddies to get inside story characters and have some fun. Starting from a favorite book or story, they improvise or script a two-person skit. Their performances can be simple or elaborate, designed to entertain each other or the whole group.

In addition to the fun of it, bringing story characters to life via role-playing or writing scripts pays dividends in children's language development. These playful ways of deepening children's connections to stories and characters also increase their comfort in using and controlling language.

Activity Structure

In preparation for this activity, older and younger children practice role-playing or scripting two-person dialogues in their own classrooms. During Buddies time, buddy pairs choose a story and create their own character dialogue. To conclude the activity, students share what they enjoyed and what was challenging about creating their skits and working with their buddy.

Planning with Your Buddy Teacher

Talk together about any role-playing, readers' theater, or scripting experiences your individual classes have had, as well as any related experiences buddies may have had, such as reading wordless books together. Talk about how those experiences relate to particular variations of Character Dialogue suggested at the end of this activity. Once buddies are experienced with Character Dialogue you may want to let them choose their own variation, but while they are new at this, suggest one structure for everyone. Think about your children and choose accordingly. For some children role-playing is a natural, but for others, the support of a script may be comforting. Decide whether props such as dolls or puppets would be helpful for your students. Consider making a list of books and stories for children to choose from; the most likely choices will be easy to read and will have two main characters and lots of dialogue. Then review the steps described below and make adjustments as needed.

Introducing the Activity with Older Students

If your students are inexperienced with the form, begin with one of the following two options for modeling role-playing or scripting.

- **Option 1: Model role-playing two story characters.** Read aloud a dialogue-rich scene between two story characters. With a student volunteer, decide who will play which character. Read the scene again and then model improvising a dialogue between the two characters – add "voice" to what the character might be feeling or thinking, extend the written scene, or create an entirely new scene that's not in the book. Highlight ways for both partners to make decisions and contribute.

- **Option 2: Model scripting a dialogue.** Use an overhead projector to project a dialogue-rich page from a story scene between two characters. With a volunteer, demonstrate making a script for the scene in either of two ways: highlight all lines of dialogue with a marker or copy them down in script form. Talk about ways for both partners to contribute to the decisions and the work. Act out the dialogue you highlighted or copied down.

- **Have partners practice.** Depending on the structure you've chosen, have partners practice either role-playing or scripting a scene from a book the class is familiar with.

- **Discuss helping younger buddies participate.** Ask students to share their thoughts and ideas about doing this with their younger buddies. How can they make decisions together? How can they help the younger buddy without taking over? How can they encourage and respond to their younger buddies' ideas?

Introducing the Activity with Younger Students

If your students are inexperienced with the form, begin with one of the following two options for modeling role-playing or scripting.

- **Option 1: Model role-playing two story characters.** Read aloud a dialogue-rich scene between two story characters. With a student volunteer, decide who will play which character. Read the scene again and then model improvising a dialogue between the two characters – add "voice" to what the characters might be feeling or thinking, extend the written scene, or create a new scene that's not in the book. Use puppets or dolls, if you like. Highlight ways for both partners to make decisions and contribute.

- **Option 2: Model scripting a dialogue.** Even if your students can't read, use an overhead projector to project a dialogue-rich page from a story scene between two characters. Read the page aloud. With a volunteer, demonstrate making a script for the scene in either of two ways: highlight all lines of dialogue with a marker or copy them down in script form. Talk about ways for both partners to contribute to the decisions and the work. Act out the dialogue you highlighted or copied down (prompt a nonreader *sotto voce*).

- **Have partners practice.** If your students are able enough readers, have them practice with a partner either role-playing or scripting a scene from a book the class is familiar with.

- **Discuss doing Character Dialogue with the older buddies.** Ask students to share their thoughts and ideas about doing this with their older buddies. How can they make decisions together? How can they give their ideas? How can they share the work?

b-mail

Have buddies send each other a note or drawing that tells what they like or don't like about being an actor.

Doing the Activity

- **Have pairs choose a story and get started.** You might want to have a collection of appropriate books for buddies to choose from. This activity will probably be more enjoyable for younger children if the books are not too difficult for them to follow.

- **Observe, make notes, respond to students.** While students are working, drop in on the partnerships and ask open-ended questions about how they are making decisions and sharing the work. If any pairs need help, model whatever the missing piece is for them. Take notes for later use in reflecting with students or your buddy teacher.

- **Have buddies discuss the experience of working together.** Invite children to talk about working with their buddies. What went well and what was hard? What could they do differently next time?

- **Invite volunteers to perform (optional).** If you have time and some dedicated hams, let them entertain the class.

Buddy Journals

Have students write or draw about their acting experience.

Reflecting

With your separate classes, have students talk about what they have learned so far about being a buddy. What suggestions do they have for revising or varying the activity the next time they do Character Dialogue with their buddies?

With your buddy teacher, discuss afterwards what went well and what was challenging. Share your observations about the activity and the students' responses to it. Consider the suggestions your classes may have made about refining the activity or trying a new variation.

Character Dialogue Variations

- **Scripts for Nonreaders.** When one of the pair is a nonreader, the older buddy reads his or her lines with dramatic flair, then quietly reads the younger buddy's lines for the younger buddy to repeat — with gusto!

- **Scripts for Nonreaders, Doubled.** If nonreaders are shy about acting, they may find strength in numbers. Double up the buddy pairs and when one of the older buddies provides the younger buddies' prompt line, have them respond as a duet.

- **Reverse Roles.** For buddies who finish early or for a follow-up meeting, have buddies reverse roles.

- **Puppet Performance.** With or without a puppet theater available, buddies can perform their dialogues as puppeteers.

- **End-less.** Buddies role-play or write and act out a conversation their characters might have at some specified time after the end of the book.

- **Across Stories.** Buddies script or improvise a dialogue bringing together two characters from different stories they have both read. What important lesson might *Ruby the Copycat* learn from *The Little Painter of Sabana Grande*? If *Ira Sleeps Over*, what might he find *Nathaniel Talking* about?

- **Prime Time.** Some buddies may enjoy an audience. Have them rehearse and present their skit live — to another buddy pair or even the whole group. Props and simple costumes can be added.

- **Shape It, Tape It.** Buddy pairs work on their dialogues, record them on audio tape, and then share them with others (including folks at home). Students can record and erase until they've shaped and taped their performance just the way they want it.

■ **Readers' Theater.** Give buddies or buddy foursomes expendable copies of a book they can highlight and challenge them to present the full story — with a narration to set the scene, and dialogue presented by minor characters as well as main characters.

Materials

- Books!
- Expendable story copies that pairs can highlight and highlighter pens (Readers' Theater)
- Materials for props and simple costumes (Prime Time)
- Tape recorders (Shape It, Tape It)
- Overhead projector for scriptwriting (optional)
- Dolls or puppets and puppets theater (optional)

Language Experience

anguage Experience is an extension to other buddy activities—it's a way for the buddies to get down in writing what they've experienced together. Whether it's the account of their zoo trip or the words to a wordless book they just read, Language Experience lets buddies tell their own story.

Buddies can dictate, write, and illustrate their experiences in a single page for a bulletin board, in a two-page spread, or in as many pages as it takes for them to make a book. Drawing on their immediate experience, memories, journal entries, or photographs, buddies discuss their ideas and write them down. And because they are creating a joint product, each time they write a Language Experience account, they build perspective-taking and collaboration abilities as well as language skills.

Activity Structure

Over the course of one or more Buddies meetings, pairs discuss an experience they've shared, decide what parts they want to tell about, and collaborate on the wording. They may each write part, the younger buddy may dictate while the older buddy scribes, or they may compose/edit out loud together while the older buddy gets it down. Their account may take the form of a newspaper article, cartoon strip, travel guide, how-to, storybook, expanded journal entry, song, or poem. Time is built in for editing or revising, and illustrations are welcome. To conclude the activity, students share their stories with others and find a place to store or display them so they can be read again and again. They reflect on what they learned and how it felt to write with their buddy.

Planning with Your Buddy Teacher

Before buddies do this together, be sure the older students have some experience writing collaboratively with a partner.

Tell each other about the writing approaches your students are accustomed to in their classroom language arts program. Talk about what approaches might naturally extend to the buddies' Language Experience. If your buddies are keeping journals, talk about how to explain Language Experience in relation to the journal writing they are already doing. For buddies' first Language Experience, choose a simple, out-of-the-classroom activity, such as a neighborhood walk or shared lunch, that can be immediately followed by the writing activity. (For later Language Experiences, you may ask pairs to pick their own past experience to write about.) Decide on an experience that will be interesting and appropriate for everyone, review the steps described below, and make adjustments as needed.

Introducing the Activity with Older Students

- **Discuss the activity's structure and purpose.** Relate the Language Experience activity to the writing students do in class and the writing they do in their buddy journals. Have students imagine what might be fun and what might be challenging about writing with their buddies. What might be learned and what might be taught?

- **Have partners practice.** Describe a format (such as a newspaper report) and have pairs of students collaborate on a short piece of writing about a recent classroom experience. Give them time to edit or revise.

- **Lead a class discussion about the partners' experiences.** What decisions did they have to make? What roles did they each take? What worked well? What was hard?

- **Have partners practice again (optional).** Depending on your students' familiarity with collaborative writing, have the same partners try another Language Experience activity; lead a discussion about what was different from their previous try.

- **Have the class anticipate working with their buddies.** Lead a discussion about how to listen actively to younger buddies and their ideas. If the younger buddies are in the pre-writing or emergent writing stage, discuss how to take dictation from a younger buddy or how to modify the dictation, letting the buddy hear exactly what gets written. Have students think of additional ways to involve the younger students in the writing and revising, as well as ways to involve them in decorating or illustrating the writing.

List the steps of the writing process used in your class. Have students imagine what they will do and what their buddy will do for each step. If you have not already done so, discuss how different perspectives can be joined in one account.

Introducing the Activity with Younger Students

- **Describe the activity.** Explain the buddy activity in relation to whatever writing children are already doing in the classroom or in their buddy journals.

- **Have children anticipate working with their buddies.** Ask children how they can share the work with their buddies. What are some things they can do? What are some things their buddies can do? What can they do together?

b-mail

If buddies have not already sent each other b-mail about the activity that this one extends, have them do so. When the Language Experience draws on past experiences, buddies can exchange teaser first lines or drawings about the experience each wants to write about (they'll later have to negotiate if they don't have the same experience in mind).

Doing the Activity

- **Buddies have an Experience together.** They turn it into a Language Experience!

- **Observe, make notes, respond to students.** If buddies need help getting started, encourage them not to worry about the final product and to begin with a list of things they know about their experience. As you circulate, ask pairs open-ended questions about how they are sharing the work. Remind students that time is built into the activity for them to make revisions. Make notes for later reflection with students or your buddy teacher.

  Have buddies who finish early find another pair and share their writing.

- **Have buddies discuss the experience of working together.** Invite children to share reflections about "writing it up" with their buddies. Ask volunteers to read their accounts to the entire group. Have students suggest ways to display or store the accounts so that they can be read over and over (especially by the younger buddies).

Buddy Journals

There's no need to have students do additional writing, but you could simply have them note the topic of their Language Experience if the writing is not itself an entry in the journals.

Reflecting

With your separate classes, invite students to share reflections about what was hard about working together, what went well, and what they learned. What could they do differently next time?

With your buddy teacher, discuss afterwards what went well and what was challenging. What suggestions did your students have for next time? What suggestions do you have?

Language Experience Variations

- **The Way We Were.** Buddies recall from memory or by looking through their journals a previous activity they enjoyed doing together and want to write about. On the plus side, buddies get to choose what to write about. On the minus side, because the details are in the past and may be hazy, writing "history" can be more challenging than writing about a fresh experience.

- **Wordless No More.** Buddies read a wordless book together, informally inventing narrative and dialogue. Then they read it again, writing it down as they go this time – either the full story or enough dialogue for a Character Dialogue presentation (see page 82).

- **Youth Rules!** Younger buddies dictate, and older buddies write as fast as they can. The dictation can be about a buddy experience or a book they read together, or it can be a story to go with a drawing the younger buddy made earlier in his or her class.

- **Imagine That.** Together buddies make up a story, and the older buddy takes the lead in polishing the writing while the younger buddy acts as illustrator. This fiction-based variation presents significant challenges; it helps for the buddies to have had experience writing the words to wordless books and scripts for dramatic activities like Character Dialogue.

- **Make-a-Book.** Buddy pairs publish their story or script in handmade books, after first making decisions together about a cover design and how to lay out and illustrate their work. When the books are completed, the whole collection can be showcased in one of the buddy classrooms or the school library.

- **Family Experience.** Younger buddies take the written product home to read to a parent or other adult and to help them begin a conversation about what the buddies did together.

Materials

- Wordless books (Wordless No More)
- Bookmaking materials (Make-a-Book)

Math Play

Math Play is built around a variety of games and explorations of pattern, probability, measurement, estimation, and number facts. Many different games will work well as a buddy activity, but the ones suggested below all model the only rule for Math Play—the activities must be noncompetitive and open-ended.

In some activities the buddies may each have different roles and different things to learn. In others they alternate roles and simply learn at their individual pace and level. The goal is for buddies to relax and have fun—with each other and with math.

Activity Structure

Each class decides separately on an open-ended, noncompetitive math activity for the buddy pairs to play together. Students then practice with their classmates the best ways to teach the game. During Buddies time, buddies partner up and teach each other the game their class practiced. To conclude the activity, students reflect on what they learned about math and about being a buddy.

Planning with Your Buddy Teacher

Each of you make a list of some noncompetitive, open-ended math games that your class already knows well. For the first time your classes get together for Math Play, decide with your buddy teacher which game from each list the buddies will play.

For subsequent Math Play meetings, let each class choose one game to play with their buddies. Limit each class to games they know well, but periodically teach new games to expand their choices. (In addition to the games suggested at the end of this activity, investigate resources such as *Family Math* [see "Materials," below], which describes activities specifically designed for older and younger age groups to do cooperatively.)

With your partner, review the steps described below, making adjustments as needed.

Introducing the Activity with Older Students

- **Describe the purpose of the activity.** Be sure students understand the idea of playing with math in a way that is fun for both buddies and that doesn't set up a competition (between the buddies or with other buddy pairs).

- **Introduce the first game buddies will play. (For later meetings, let the class choose.)** Give partners a chance to play the game and remember how it works.

- **Have students practice explaining the game.** Have students practice explaining the game to a partner. What about the directions may be hard? What about the math may be hard?

- **Have a volunteer model how to explain the game.** Take the role of the younger buddy and present yourself as a naive learner.

- **Have students discuss their responsibilities.** Have students anticipate how to keep their buddies interested in the game. What do they hope their younger buddies will learn? How do they want their younger buddies to feel?

Introducing the Activity with Younger Students

- **Describe the buddy activity.** Explain that buddies will play a math game that is fun for both of them.

- **Introduce the first game buddies will play. (For later meetings, let the class choose.)** Give partners a chance to play the game and remember how it works.

- **Have the class discuss how to explain the game to their buddies.** What may be confusing to explain?

- **Have students practice explaining the game.** Ask partners to take turns explaining the game.

- **Have a volunteer model explaining the game.** Take the role of the older buddy and present yourself as a naive learner.

- **Have students discuss their responsibilities.** What will students need to do when they are the teacher of the game? What will they need to do when their buddy is the teacher of the game? What will both buddies have to do when they play the games?

b-mail

Have buddies send each other a hint about the math activity they have planned for each other.

Doing the Activity

- **Observe, make notes, respond to students.** Circulate among the pairs. Check for understanding of the game directions and math concepts by asking open-ended questions. Note topics for later student reflection and any issues to bring up with your buddy teacher.

- **Have buddies reflect on their experience.** Invite children to talk about how it went. What was fun? What was hard? What did they learn?

Buddy Journals

Invite students to make a record of their Math Play experience in their journals.

Reflecting

With your separate classes, have students talk about what they are learning about being buddies and what is hard.

With your buddy teacher, discuss afterwards what went well and what was challenging. Were these math activities ones that students would benefit from repeating? Discuss any observations you or your partner made about individual buddy pairs and what interventions, if any, might be called for in the future.

Math Play Variations

- **Pattern-Block Symmetry.** Buddies take turns adding pattern blocks to a symmetrical design they are creating jointly. Buddies can alternate going first and inventing the design or going second and mirroring the design. Both younger and older buddies explore design, pattern, and symmetry.

- **Geoboard Match.** Buddies take turns creating a design on a geoboard for the other buddy to copy on a second geoboard. The "originating" buddy can create the design in stages or all at once. Younger buddies explore shapes and patterns. Older buddies try to figure out what is hard and easy for their buddy and how to create designs that stretch but do not frustrate the younger child.

- **Hidden Structures.** One buddy tries to duplicate a hidden block structure that the other buddy is building or has built. The "originating" buddy watches over a partition that separates the two structures and describes block by block how the "duplicating" buddy should proceed. Buddies alternate roles, and both buddies learn about spatial relationships, as well as how to give clear instructions and how to be patient and encouraging. To vary the challenge, limit or expand the number and variety of blocks. To add to the challenge, have the originating buddy give directions without seeing the result until the end.

- **Paper Airplane Trials.** Each pair of buddies designs two or three different paper airplanes, flies each design a predetermined number of times, measures and records the distance of each flight, and makes a hypothesis about which design is most aerodynamic and why. Buddy pairs then make a report to the whole group or to another buddy pair. The group or foursome tries to determine if their aggregate data support or confound the conclusions arrived at by individual buddy pairs. Both younger and older buddies learn about measurement and keeping records. Older buddies also explore drawing conclusions and making hypotheses.

- **Probability Dice.** Buddy pairs throw two dice to explore probability. They record each roll of the dice in either of two ways (you decide before introducing the game).

    Option 1. By recording the dice rolls on a graph-paper grid numbered from two to twelve, the pairs plot the shape of the data as a bar graph. Younger students explore graphing and practice adding dice. Older students practice creating bar graphs and informally explore probability.

Option 2. By recording the dice rolls for each sum with tally marks, the pairs practice counting, adding, and multiplying sets of five. Younger students explore chunking numbers. Older students informally explore probability. To increase the challenge, students can change the number of tally marks in a set, practicing with multiples of three, seven, or four, for example.

■ **Just a Minute!** Buddies take turns estimating how many times the other buddy can repeat a given movement or activity (such as hopping or writing the alphabet) in a minute. Let the pairs make up their own challenges — that way buddy pairs won't compete with each other and students can focus on sharpening their estimation skills.

■ **Decahedron-Die Sums.** In a one-minute period, one buddy throws a decahedron die repeatedly, and the other records the running sum. In each consecutive one-minute period, the buddies alternate roles. The objective is for buddies to help each other beat their personal records for adding a running sum. Younger and older students increase their facility with number facts. Challenge may be introduced by changing the operation to subtraction, from a fixed amount such as 100; or by having children progress from writing each algorithm in a lengthening column to recording sums only, then to adding mentally (and aloud).

Materials

- Game equipment for two games. Depending on your resources, provide each buddy pair with the equipment for both games; or provide buddy foursomes with the equipment for both games and ask the buddy pairs to trade games halfway through the period. If game equipment is particularly scarce and students are very familiar with the game rules, establish stations for a larger variety of games requiring fewer sets of equipment at each station.

- *Family Math,* published by the Lawrence Hall of Science at the University of California at Berkeley, 510-642-1823 (optional)

Artists Together

As a twosome, buddies who are Artists Together benefit from an older buddy who may be more accomplished and a younger buddy who may be more daring. As a creative combo, they have the potential to inspire each other and improve on what either might have come up with alone.

Whether exploring with fingerpaints or learning perspective, buddy artists get smocked and go creative. They can work side by side and then combine their efforts, or they can collaborate in more interdependent ways. They can take the lead in teaching technique or take a chance in "messing around." The idea is to enjoy the companionship of Artists Together.

Activity Structure

Buddy classes take turns hosting art activities. In their separate classes, older or younger students decide on a way to be Artists Together. If they will be introducing their buddies to a new project or technique, students practice ahead of time in their own classrooms. During Buddies time, the buddies share materials and maybe a product as they work on the chosen art project. To conclude, buddies show their work to and exchange ideas with other pairs, perhaps contribute to a group "museum" or display, and take some time to reflect on how it was to work together.

Planning with Your Buddy Teacher

Before gathering activity suggestions from your students, agree on some general parameters that you both are comfortable with. For example, how much mess can you tolerate, and how long and involved a project are you ready for? Or are you open to waiting and seeing what your students propose? Once the hosting class has a plan, decide how and where buddies will work together: Can they spread out in one or both classrooms, or would it be better to work with the art teacher and use the art room? With your partner, review the steps described below and make adjustments as needed.

Introducing the Activity with Older Students

- **If your class hosts, describe the purpose of buddy art.** Help students understand that the purpose is to give buddies a chance to enjoy an art project together. Help students understand why they will not want to intimidate their buddies with a complicated project or compete for the "best" work.

- **Have students brainstorm ideas for buddy art projects.** Ask students for their ideas and list them on the board. Make suggestions, if necessary, or ask questions to get things started: What kind of artwork does this class enjoy doing? What would be fun to make with buddies? What kind of project would the buddies enjoy? Help the children narrow their ideas down and choose one.

- **Have partners practice teaching the activity (optional).** Have partners practice the activity, explaining how to do it as if to a younger buddy. What might be hard to explain? What can each buddy do to share in the project?

- **Have the class discuss how to work with their buddies.** How can students share ideas and the work without taking over?

- **If your class is invited . . .** Explain in general terms the activity the younger buddies have planned. Have students imagine their role as the guest (and the learner, perhaps).

Introducing the Activity with Younger Students

- **If your class hosts, introduce the idea of buddy art.** Let students know that buddy art can be as simple as drawing together or as complicated as making a puppet together.

- **Have students think about art projects they love.** Ask the class to brainstorm their favorite art projects. List their ideas on the board.

- **Help them choose an activity to share with their buddies.** Have the children imagine sharing one of these art projects with their buddies. Is there one that stands out? Is there a particular technique they'd like to teach their buddies? Maybe there's a project that would be particularly fun for everyone?

- **Have partners practice teaching the activity (optional).** If the children settle on an activity they want to teach their older buddies, have them practice it with a partner, explaining the directions as if they were explaining them to their older buddies.

- **Discuss what it will be like doing the activity with the buddies.** After they practice, have students talk about what went well and what was challenging. Ask students to share ideas about how to introduce this art activity to their buddies and how to do their part.

- **If your class is invited . . .** Explain in general terms the activity the older buddies have planned. Have students imagine their role as the guest (and the learner, perhaps).

b-mail

Have students in the host class send artistic invitations to their buddies.

Doing the Activity

- **Observe, make notes, respond to students.** As you circulate among the pairs, ask students how they are sharing ideas, making decisions, or sharing the work. Make notes for use in later reflections with students or your buddy teacher.

- **Have buddies discuss their experience.** Invite children to talk about how it went. What was fun? What was messy or hard? What would they like to do differently next time? Welcome suggestions for what buddies can do with their work — perhaps have a museum walk around the room or create a hallway display? (See "Buddy Museum," below, as one possibility.)

Buddy Journals

Invite buddies to write or draw about their art experience.

Reflecting

With your separate classes, talk with students about what they are learning about being a buddy. What suggestions do they have for future buddy art experiences?

With your buddy teacher, discuss afterwards what went well and what was challenging. Share your observations about the activity and the students' responses to it. Consider the suggestions your classes may have made about future buddy art projects.

Ways to Be Artists Together

- **Side by Side.** Buddies can take comfort in working side by side on their own artwork and then combining it — as in a collage or book. Afterwards, buddies can share and explain their work in foursomes.

- **Let Me Show You.** For this activity, either buddy teaches the other a new or special art project, technique, or way of working together as artists. Try string painting, origami, coil clay, paper weaving, or even thumbprint drawing.

- **Messing Around.** This could be a relaxed, joint exploration of painting, collage-making, drawing, working with clay, etc. Buddies are free to "mess around" side by side or together to see what they can come up with. Afterward, buddies can share their ideas, experiments, and products with other buddy pairs.

- **Buddy Museum.** Buddies turn one or both classrooms into a "buddy museum" to display their artwork. Together, the two classes figure out how they want to display their work, whom they want to invite, and what they'd like to write or tell about their art projects for visitors. Parents could be invited, as well as other classes and staff members.

- **Buddy Collage Mural.** This congenial buddy art project can combine the efforts of two buddy pairs or the whole group — depending on the length of the butcher paper! The butcher paper background can be blank or can define an environment (such as a cityscape or ocean reef). Individuals or pairs make people, plants, vehicles, chairs, windows, etc. for the overall scene, cut them out, and glue them on the butcher paper in ways that interact with the other cutouts already glued on (and to come).

Materials

- Art supplies of all kinds (depending on the activity)
- Smocks
- Water or access to a sink

Portfolio Sharing

Portfolio Sharing is a form of buddy "show and tell" that allows children to take pride in their accomplishments. It can also be a time when buddies try out works-in-progress and respond to each other in the role of a thoughtful questioner. Together, buddies investigate classroom work they've chosen to share—drawings, stories, math projects, science reports—and bring each other into their thinking and learning. By asking "Why did you choose this?" or "What is your favorite part?" or "What would make this part clearer?" and then listening to the answer, buddies treat each other as learners doing authentic work—because they are!

Portfolio Sharing allows children to identify and appreciate their own successes. It can also reinforce the idea that work-in-progress is a puzzle to solve, not an embarrassment or a failure. And the support and practice buddies provide for each other will go a long way toward preparing them to present their classroom portfolios and other work to parents and other adults at home.

Activity Structure

In their separate classrooms, each student chooses one or two favorite portfolio products, or a special project just completed, or a work-in-progress that feels promising or could use a second opinion. When the buddies get together, they take turns investigating each other's work by asking open-ended questions about what the creator has learned, feels satisfied with, or is mulling over. To conclude the activity, buddies reflect on what they learned by exchanging the stories behind their work.

Planning with Your Buddy Teacher

Because it is important for students to truly choose the work they share and to feel good about their choice, don't try to do this activity before they have accumulated a range of products and the confidence to share works-in-progress.

Talk together about how each of you uses portfolios or would like to use them. Discuss the ways this activity represents or varies from your approaches. It could be confusing, for example, if students in one class select from works-in-progress and students in the other class expect only polished work to be shared. Decide how to align the activity with both of your approaches. Then review the steps described below and make any necessary adjustments.

Introducing the Activity with Older Students

- **For classes that are new to portfolios . . .** Talk about your goals for portfolios – for the classroom and for work with the buddies. Have students store selected work in a folder or special drawer over the course of several weeks. If you use folders, invite students to decorate them.

- **For classes that already use portfolios in some way . . .** Make sure that a variety of projects in a variety of subject areas are included.

- **Have students choose items to share.** Distribute portfolios and have students select one or two finished pieces to show their buddies. Have them write themselves notes about why they selected each piece. (You might want to delay introducing the routines for works-in-progress until buddies are comfortable with the routines for finished pieces.)

- **Model asking open-ended questions for portfolio sharing.** Invite a volunteer to show you something from his or her portfolio. Begin with a question like "Why did you choose this to show me?" If the student then describes something that is finished and a source of satisfaction, your next questions should reflect that. For example, if the student says, "This is the first time I tried to write something funny. It makes me laugh," you might respond, "What did you think would be hard about writing something funny?" or "Read me the part that makes you laugh." Additional follow-up questions could go in the direction of "How did you actually get the idea for that part?" or "What did you have to do to get it exactly the way you wanted it?" The point is to accept the author's judgment and probe the process.

At a later time when you are modeling response to a work-in-progress, your questions should help the student articulate his or her ideas or concerns about it. You would still begin the conversation with as open a question as possible, such as "Tell me why you chose this piece." You might then follow up with questions such as "Tell me about the part you think is the best and then let's compare it with the part you're not happy with," or "How would you say that if you were talking instead of writing?" or "Where does it get confusing, exactly?" Although the student has invited feedback from someone else, the point is to ask questions that help uncover more of his or her own ideas.

- **Have partners practice.** Let partners practice asking each other open-ended questions that show interest in the other's work but don't pass judgment on it.

- **Brainstorm a list of open-ended portfolio probes.** Have students describe some of the questions they tried with their partners. Which ones were helpful? Which ones didn't go anywhere? Which ones were too much like giving an opinion? Which ones showed that the person was interested? List the successful questions for use with buddies (and in the classroom and to send home with students' portfolios).

- **Have students take their younger buddy's perspective.** Encourage students to imagine how their buddies might feel about their work and showing it to someone older. Help them see that some may naturally feel proud and others may be shy or nervous. Ask for ideas about helping buddies feel confident and successful.

Introducing the Activity with Younger Students

- **For classes that are new to portfolios . . .** Talk about your goals for portfolios – for the classroom and for work with the buddies. Have students store selected work in a folder or special drawer over the course of several weeks. If you use folders, invite students to decorate them.

- **For classes that already use portfolios in some way . . .** Make sure that a variety of projects in a variety of subject areas are included.

- **Model choosing two or three things from a portfolio.** From a volunteer's portfolio, choose two or three things that are finished. (Delay introducing the routines for works-in-progress until students are comfortable with the routines for finished pieces.) Help the volunteer think out loud about what he or she would want to tell a buddy about each selection.

- **Have partners help each other choose items to share.** Ask partners to tell each other why they chose each item.

- **Model asking open-ended questions for portfolio sharing.** Invite a volunteer to show you something from his or her portfolio. Ask questions such as "Why did you choose this to show me?" "What is your favorite part?" "What was the hardest part?" "What did you learn?" and "Tell me about this."

At a later time when you model asking questions about works-in-progress, ask questions such as "Why did you decide you weren't really finished with this?"

"Who can you imagine reading/looking at this?" and "Why are you willing to try harder to finish this?"

- **Have partners practice.** Let partners practice asking each other open-ended questions that show interest in the other's work but don't pass judgment on it.

- **Brainstorm a list of open-ended portfolio probes.** Have students describe some of the questions they tried with their partners. Which ones were helpful? Which ones showed that the person asking the question was interested? List the successful questions for use with buddies (and in the classroom and to send home with students' portfolios).

- **Have students imagine their role as their buddy's audience.** Encourage students to imagine how their buddies might feel about their work and showing it to someone younger. Help them see that some may naturally feel proud and others may even be shy. What could they say to let their buddy know that they appreciate being able to see the work he or she has done?

- **Have students imagine their role as the presenter.** Ask students to imagine how they want their buddies to act when they show them their work. What could they say to their buddies to let them know this?

b-mail

Have children send b-mail to tell their buddies about something they have been saving in their portfolio to share.

Doing the Activity

- **Observe, make notes, respond to students.** As you observe, help buddies who are having a hard time. Model and then ask students to try out an open-ended question. Circulate and make notes for later reflection with the students or your buddy teacher.

- **Have buddies discuss their experience.** Invite children to share reflections about how they felt sharing their work with their buddies and what they learned.

Buddy Journals

Have students write or draw about something they learned about the buddy's work or their own work.

Reflecting

With your separate classes, have students talk about what they are learning about being a buddy and what they are learning about their own work.

With your buddy teacher, discuss afterwards what went well and what was challenging. Talk about ways to build on this activity, both in class and during Buddies time. Plan when to repeat the portfolio sharing. Decide whether to include works-in-progress; consider what kind of preparation that would require.

Portfolio Sharing Variations

- **The Most.** Change the selection criteria. For example, one week buddies select the thing in their portfolio that was the most fun, the next week they select the thing that was the most surprising, the next week they select the thing that was the most trouble but worth it, or that caused them to learn the most, or that they would be most proud to show a parent.

- **Buddy Biographies.** Buddy classes each learn about the life of a special person. When the buddy pairs get together, students introduce each other to the person each of them learned about.

- **Learning Projects.** Older buddies share a learning project they have worked on. The "teaching" buddies first find out what the younger buddies already know about the topic and what they would like to know. They then present their projects, pointing out the things the buddies already knew, the things the buddies said they wanted to know, and new things that the buddies didn't even know they wanted to know!

- **Buddy Editing.** Younger buddies choose a piece of writing they would like to polish. Older buddies read the piece out loud to the author and implement the author's suggested changes.

- **The Whole Enchilada.** At the end of a semester or year, buddies show each other their complete portfolios — everything that survived the winnowing process. They talk about what they have learned and how they have grown.

- **Parent Practice.** Together, buddies practice talking about selections from their portfolios (or the whole enchilada) in preparation for sharing their work at home or in a parent conference at school.

Materials

- A folder or other portfolio container for each student
- Each student's poems, stories, reports, drawings, collages, projects, inventions, solutions, and other portfolio selections
- A list of open-ended questions to ask about portfolio selections (optional)

STEPPING OUT

THE OPPORTUNITY to step out together – to the lunchroom or the symphony – can add an exciting dimension to students' buddy relationships. Whether they go near or far, for a short time or a whole day, children are likely to get a thrill out of discovering both new and familiar places and experiences with buddies in hand.

The activities that follow include some that transform routine parts of school life into special buddy activities, some that are out-and-out outings, and some that require a long-term commitment and yield long-lasting satisfaction. As you explore the various ways for buddies to step out, you and your students are bound to come up with dozens of your own ideas to add to the ones here.

- **We Go Together**
- **Field-Trip Buddies**
- **Green Team**
- **Working for a Cause**

We Go Together

We Go Together is a no-fuss way to transform ordinary aspects of "life at school" into a special Buddies time. Pair up your buddy classes and let partners go together—to the library, to the cafeteria, to the playground, to an assembly, to music class.

We Go Together activities are a boon for teachers as well as the children. The younger buddies have personal chaperones, and the older children are on their best behavior in situations where they might otherwise be at their worst. For a first We Go Together jaunt, try Lunch Bunch, which can be as simple as having buddies eat together, or Library Buddies, where a visit to the library means sharing a book with your buddy when you get there.

Activity Structure

In their separate classrooms, older and younger children share ideas about a familiar school activity they'd like to liven up by doing it with their buddies. During Buddies time, both classes enjoy the activity with its new Buddies twist. To conclude, students reflect on what they enjoyed about being with their buddies and what they learned from the experience.

Planning with Your Buddy Teacher

Before gathering suggestions from your students, share ideas about We Go Together activities you both agree would be fun and manageable for everyone. Consider both self-contained activities (such as going to lunch together), as well as activities that could lend themselves to joint follow-up projects (such as going to an assembly about fire safety and making fire-safety posters together). Your shared understanding of the parameters of successful activities will guide students' discussions of ways to go together with their buddies. Review the steps described below and make adjustments as needed.

Introducing the Activity with Older Students

WHEN YOUR CLASS IS HOSTING . . .

- **Have students discuss and choose a way We Go Together.** Ask students for their ideas about activities that they might enjoy in a new way – with their buddies. From a brainstorm list, have students choose an activity to try.

- **Have students visualize doing the buddy activity.** Talk with your students about what it's like to do to this activity as a class. Then have them visualize doing it with their buddies. What will be different? What will be fun? What will be hard? Invite specific suggestions about how to make the activity interesting and enjoyable for everyone. List students' ideas on the board and chose one or more specific approaches to try as a class.

- **Have students talk about taking responsibility.** Have students anticipate the ways they will be responsible for their younger buddies – whether for a playground excursion, in the lunchroom, or in transit to and from a school performance. How can they help their buddies feel comfortable and safe?

WHEN YOUR CLASS HAS BEEN INVITED . . .

- **RSVP!** If the younger children have issued an invitation for a joint activity, ask students what it might be like to be guests of the younger buddies. Have them talk about the ways in which being guests might require a change in the role older buddies usually play. Ask students to consider how to help their little buddies feel confident about taking the lead. Finally, have students reply to their buddies' invitation.

Introducing the Activity with Younger Students

WHEN YOUR CLASS HAS BEEN INVITED . . .

- **Describe the activity.** Describe or, if possible, have one or two visitors from the buddy class describe the joint activity the older buddies have planned.

- **Have students visualize doing the buddy activity.** Talk with your students about what it's like to do this activity as a class. Then have them visualize doing it with their buddies. What will be different? What will be fun? What will be hard? What can their buddy help them with?

- **RSVP!** Have students reply to their buddies' invitation.

WHEN YOUR CLASS IS HOSTING . . .

- **Have students discuss and choose a way We Go Together.** The children will surely have their own ideas about ways We Go Together. Why not have them take the lead? Once the class chooses an activity, talk together about what it means to "host." What might be different about having older buddies as your guests? What can you look forward to? What could you plan? Help students think about ways to make the activity enjoyable for the older students.

b-mail

Have one class invite the other, or have each buddy create a personal invitation to his or her partner. Don't forget to RSVP.

Doing the Activity

- **Observe, make notes, respond to students.** During the activity, notice ways buddies are or are not enjoying themselves and taking responsibility. Ask questions if a buddy pair is having difficulty. Make notes about the activity and students' response to it for later reflection with students or your buddy teacher.

- **Have buddies discuss their experience.** Invite children to discuss what they enjoyed about being outside the classroom together. Ask what challenges or rough spots they encountered and what they learned as a result.

Buddy Journals

Invite students to write or draw about their experience in their buddy journals.

Reflecting

With your separate classes, invite students to reflect on what they learned about being a buddy from this experience. What would they like to do differently next time? Do students have ideas about how to modify or improve the activity? What other We Go Together activities would they like to try with their buddies?

With your buddy teacher, discuss what went well and what was challenging. Could the activity be productively tweaked? How well prepared were the students? Discuss any observations you made about individual buddy pairs and what interventions, if any, might be called for in the future. Share any suggestions your students made about ways to modify this activity or buddy up in the future.

Places We Go Together

■ **Library Buddies.** At the school library, older buddies read their younger buddy a favorite book, or both buddies read to each other from a book each has chosen. They talk about their favorite parts, their ideas, and their questions. For a read-aloud to the entire group, younger buddies may enjoy snuggling up on their buddies' laps.

■ **Lunch Bunch.** Buddies walk hand in hand to the cafeteria, pick up a milk together, find a spot to sit down and eat, and maybe even share dessert.

■ **Assembly Time.** Older buddies escort their younger buddies to a schoolwide assembly and sit with them. If the occasion calls for it, buddies work together on a follow-up activity, such as a thank-you letter to the performers or a related art project.

■ **Playground Buddies.** Buddies hang out together on the playground, show each other their favorite spots, and join in activities together. Older buddies take on the role of looking after their younger buddies; they might also organize an activity that a whole group of buddies could enjoy.

■ **The Creative Side.** For this, buddies go to art or music time together. Older and younger buddies teach each other a favorite song, learn a new one together, or work together on an exciting art project.

Materials

● Materials will vary with the activity

Field-Trip Buddies

Field-Trip Buddies takes buddies on special excursions beyond the school grounds and outside of the everyday routine. Whether a field trip is simple or involved, structured or open-ended, buddies are sure to enjoy exploring the world together and sharing what they learn.

For older buddies, a field trip is a special challenge. Not only do the older children look out for their buddies, they also act as learning mentors and teachers by sharing their own observations and drawing out those of their buddies.

Activity Structure

Students learn about the proposed field trip in their separate classrooms and brainstorm ideas about how to make it a special day for their buddies. Following the trip itself, buddies can work on connection activities together back at school. To conclude, students reflect on their experience, what they learned, and what they enjoyed about going somewhere with their buddies.

Planning with Your Buddy Teacher

Share ideas for places buddies could go together and how the trip might build on something they are learning about at school. Decide on a destination or a process for involving students in choosing a destination, how to handle the arrangements, and what kind of pre- and post-trip activities the children might work on together. Consider including a picnic lunch or some unstructured time at a convenient playground as part of the trip. Review the steps described below together and make adjustments as needed.

Introducing the Activity with Older Students

- **Let students know they will be going on a field trip.** If the trip is already set, share the plans with students. Tell them some information about the destination or event – details of a particular museum exhibit, the title of the story the play is based on, what they can look for on the dairy farm, etc.

- **Have students find out more.** Have partners or small groups investigate the destination or event and report back to the class.

- **Hold class planning meetings (optional).** An alternative to a teacher-planned trip is to let students in on the process. For example, they could get involved from the beginning in choosing a destination – in researching and gathering information, in analyzing costs and benefits, and in building consensus. If having students generate the list of options seems too ambitious, you could provide a set of options for them to choose among. Guide students to think about possible differences between a destination they might choose for themselves and one they might choose for themselves and their buddies.

- **Have students imagine taking the field trip with their buddies.** Have them chat with a partner about what it might be like: What are you looking forward to? What might be interesting? What might be particularly challenging? What do you hope to share with your buddy?

- **Discuss ideas for making the trip special for younger buddies.** Lead a class discussion about the ways in which the children can help make the experience special for their buddies. Share ideas about how to help buddies feel comfortable and safe, learn something new, and have fun, as well as whatever else is on students' minds.

- **Discuss the responsibilities of the trip.** Ask the students to think about how they can act responsibly on the trip and help be responsible for their buddies.

Introducing the Activity with Younger Buddies

- **Describe the field-trip plan.** Let everyone know about the trip the two buddy classes will take. Share whatever information you can about where they're going and what they'll be doing.

- **Interview a veteran.** If the field trip is a common destination for your school, invite students from other classes who have made the trip before to be interviewed by your students. Have your students prepare some questions in advance.

- **Invite stories of similar excursions.** Some children are bound to speak up about a family outing to the zoo, a special scouting trip to the museum, or a play they saw last year. Invite everyone to share their stories.

- **Help students imagine being on the field trip with their buddies.** Have the children imagine going on the trip with their buddies: What do you think you will enjoy? What might be challenging? What would you like your buddy to know ahead of time?

- **Ask the children how they can help their buddies during the trip.** Invite students to talk with a partner about how they could help their buddy during the trip. Ask volunteers to share their thoughts and ideas with the rest of the class.

b-mail

Have buddies send each other notes or drawings about what they're looking forward to or what they hope to learn.

Doing the Activity

Observe, make notes, respond to students. Throughout the trip, circulate and talk with the buddies. Make notes about your observations for later reflection with students or your buddy teacher.

Back in School

Invite children to talk about how it went. What went well? What was challenging? What did they learn? Ask for suggestions for connection activities the buddies might enjoy doing.

Buddy Journals

Have buddies enter the story of their field trip in their journals. You may want to suggest doing a "scrapbook-style page" if students have picked up any mementos, brochures, or postcards along the way. A compilation of entries from all the journals could make an interesting buddy book.

Reflecting

With your separate classes, invite students to reflect on what they learned from this experience about being a buddy. What would they like to do differently next time? How could the field trip itself be modified or improved?

With your buddy teacher, discuss what went well and what was challenging. Share observations about the process of planning, organizing, and stepping out on the trip. Discuss students' ideas for modifying or improving the trip.

Field-Trip Variations

■ **Museum Buddies.** Buddy pairs tour a museum, guided by a "discovery journal" — a collection of questions, clues, and activities created by you, or you and the students, ahead of time. At the aquarium, for example, buddies might be asked to find, identify, and illustrate their favorite fish.

■ **A Day at the Zoo.** In small, chaperoned groups, buddies monkey around at the zoo. The trip can be lots of fun while also incorporating important academic goals. Buddies' zoo experiences could begin or end a unit on habitats, for example, or buddies could choose a particular animal or two to learn more about.

■ **Walkabout.** The two buddy classes go together on foot for a local excursion — a walk around the neighborhood, a visit to a local monument, a through-the-fence viewing of a construction site, or a trip to anything else of interest near the school. Parents may be especially helpful in setting up behind-the-scenes visits to work sites.

■ **Pumpkin Patch.** Buddies go together to a farm or pumpkin patch to enjoy autumn and pick out a pumpkin together. Younger buddies are able to enjoy having an older and bigger friend along — a friend who can help lift an even bigger pumpkin!

■ **On Stage.** Together, the two buddy classes head off to a matinee performance or children's theater. Is the production based on a book the buddies could read together? After the show it may be possible for the buddies to interview a cast member, the director, the stage manager, the lighting director, etc., asking questions they generated prior to the field trip.

Materials

● Materials will vary, depending on the excursion

● Permission slips — of course!

● Extra chaperones, as needed

● Discovery journals (Museum Buddies)

Green Team

As a Green Team, buddy classes work together to make the school, playground, or surrounding community a little bit greener or a little bit cleaner—and an all-around nicer place to be. Green Team activities can also be a way for students to move science and social studies out of the classroom and into the "real" world.

Green Team activities may spring from students' concerns about their immediate environment, a pet project of yours that students share, or an extension of classroom study. A unit on plants or tides, for example, could lead to planting a garden or cleaning a beach. Mostly, Green Team activities should be a fun way for everyone to learn about and pitch in to improve their surroundings.

Activity Structure

One class invites the other to join them in an activity they have spent some time thinking about. In either class, students learn about a possible Green Team challenge, decide they would like to do something about it, and then brainstorm ways they and their buddies can work together. The initiating class then presents their ideas to their buddy class, invites their comments or suggestions, and decides with them how to work together. During Buddies time – possibly over several weeks – both classes get involved in cleaning up, planting, recycling, conserving, or whatever else the project demands. To conclude the activity, students reflect on how it feels to take responsibility for the environment around them, what they learned, and how it was to work with their buddies.

Planning with Your Buddy Teacher

The impetus for doing this activity can come from the students, the two of you, or both; it can originate with the younger buddies or the older buddies. If students present a concern and are motivated to act, help them get organized. If you want to engage students in a project you feel enthusiastic about, or you see a natural way to combine a classroom topic and a Green Team activity, take the lead.

Well before a topic gets discussed with students, discuss in general what kinds of projects your classes might do and how the two of you want your classes to work together. This will be a whole-class pairing, not strictly a buddy pairing. Later, when an activity has been identified, talk about specific ways the classes can work together and how to let students take responsibility. Also talk about the possibility of the project going schoolwide and how you might communicate about it with the rest of the staff.

The most important planning you do will be in responding to students' goals and ideas — in helping them shape their involvement so that they feel a genuine commitment to the project.

Introducing the Activity with Older Students When They Take the Lead

- **Talk about the idea.** In the case of a school cleanup project, for example, invite students to reflect on the school's environment, how it affects them, and how they think it might affect others. If the activity will extend a classroom study, invite students to consider how their enthusiasm for a particular topic or issue could result in a tangible contribution to the school or wider community.

- **Host a special visitor or "expert" (optional).** Depending on the project, you may want to invite a guest — such as a gardener if you will be planting things or an oceanographer if you will be cleaning up near tide pools. Invite the buddy class and let children sit with their buddies.

- **Have students brainstorm the steps they will have to take.** As students share their ideas, list them on the board. Review the list, helping students make the suggestions specific, eliminate those that are impractical, choose the ones they will focus on, and sequence them.

- **Introduce the idea of working with younger buddies.** Invite students' ideas about how to include their buddies. What specific ways can the buddies help? Are there particular jobs that can be done by subteams of two or four sets of buddy pairs? What can the older students do to make sure the younger students feel responsible? What can they do so the younger students do not feel bossed around?

- **Arrange for the buddy class to consider participating.** Describe the proposed activity to your buddy teacher. Decide whether the buddy teacher or members of your class will introduce the idea to the younger students.

Introducing the Activity with Younger Students When They Take the Lead

- **Talk about the idea.** Facilitate a discussion about the project idea and help students visualize what they could do. Encourage them to ask questions.

- **Host a special visitor or "expert" (optional).** Invite a special guest who can make the idea more concrete for children. Include your buddy class and let children sit with their buddies.

- **Have students brainstorm all the jobs in the project.** List their ideas on the board.

- **Discuss sharing this project with buddies.** Ask students to imagine working on this project with their buddies. What could the younger students do? What could the older students do? What could they do together?

- **Arrange for the buddy class to consider participating.** Describe the proposed project to your buddy teacher. Decide whether the buddy teacher or members of your class will introduce the idea to the older students.

b-mail

This is an activity for whole-class b-mail. Have the initiating class send their buddy class an invitation to join them in a Green Team project. If the invited class agrees to join in, have them send a whole-class reply.

Doing the Activity

- **Have students create visible Green Team spirit (optional).** Invite students to create a design or logo for their project. Have them make bright sashes, buttons, or armbands to wear when they go to work.

- **Help the students get organized.** Turn over as much responsibility as possible to the students and monitor their progress without taking over.

- **Hold joint and separate class meetings.** If the activity will extend over several weeks, hold regular meetings to assess how things are going with both the project and the buddies. Have students, in their separate classes and with the classes together, reflect on their goals, processes, and behaviors. What are they learning? What do they want to change or improve?

- **Observe and facilitate.** Depending on the scope of the activity, as you observe and facilitate you may also want to take photographs of the Green Team in action. Students are likely to feel proud of their efforts and may appreciate visual documentation for a scrapbook, hallway display, or their buddy journals.

Buddy Journals

With an ongoing activity, the cumulative entries in the buddy journals can be especially rich in narrative and reflection. At the conclusion of the activity, classes may want to compile a buddies' book about their experience, to which individual students contribute quotes from their journals.

Reflecting

In addition to the class meetings you hold during the activity, when the project is complete have students take a long view of the whole effort. How did it feel to participate? What have they learned or especially enjoyed? What was it like teaming up with their buddies? What effect do they think the project has had on the outside community?

With your buddy teacher, take a long view of the effort. Discuss what went well and what was challenging. Talk about possible improvements or variations for the next time!

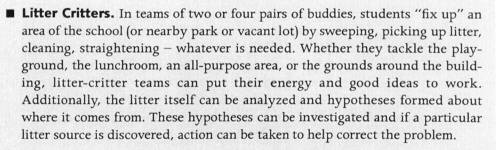

Green Team Variations

- **Litter Critters.** In teams of two or four pairs of buddies, students "fix up" an area of the school (or nearby park or vacant lot) by sweeping, picking up litter, cleaning, straightening – whatever is needed. Whether they tackle the playground, the lunchroom, an all-purpose area, or the grounds around the building, litter-critter teams can put their energy and good ideas to work. Additionally, the litter itself can be analyzed and hypotheses formed about where it comes from. These hypotheses can be investigated and if a particular litter source is discovered, action can be taken to help correct the problem.

- **Recycle That!** The two buddy classes work together to start a recycling program at school or to add new energy to an existing program. Students can arrange for containers, pickup, signs, posters, and other details to make this effort a well-organized and well-publicized success.

- **Green Thumb.** Buddy classes work together to propose or plan a new school garden or in small teams to maintain and improve an existing garden area. Buddies can add a new sign, paint a fence, tend to the flowers, water, weed, or even start (and taste) a vegetable patch. In a more urban setting, buddies can create window boxes, terrariums, or an indoor garden together. As an extension, buddies might also create and maintain a school compost pile.

- ■ **Community Green.** The two buddy classes sign up together to participate in a planned event in the community — a beach cleanup day, flower planting at a nursing home, a park improvement day. Since most such events are scheduled for weekends, why not invite families as well?

- ■ **Go Schoolwide.** For any Green Team activities, consider inviting two other buddy classes or the entire school to participate. Everyone will be able to pitch in for a recycling drive, the creation of a new garden, or a special day in the local community. The buddy classes can work together to plan and create flyers, posters, invitations, schedules, and the like.

Materials

- Brooms, mops, sponges, rakes, litterbags, etc., as needed
- Scrapbook or poster board for a display about the project
- Camera (optional)
- Supplies for buttons, armbands, or sashes (optional)

Working for a Cause

Working for a Cause is a spirited way for children to get involved in the world around them. By identifying the needs of others and acting from their own compassion, children experience themselves as caring and efficacious—people who are able to make a difference. When they work with a buddy class, children also experience the power of a group effort.

Working for a Cause can be a one-time activity or a project that lasts several weeks. Whether the cause involves contributing to a specific relief effort, organizing a food or clothing drive for homeless people, or simply sending messages of hope or concern, the process of identifying a need, deciding on goals, and then taking a course of action is rich with possibilities for growth.

Activity Structure

One class invites the other to join them in an activity they have spent some time thinking about. In either class, students learn about a serious need in their community or beyond, decide they would like to do something about it, and then brainstorm ways they and their buddies can make a difference. The initiating class presents their ideas to their buddy class, invites their comments or suggestions, and decides with them how to work together. During Buddies time both classes get involved in raising money, collecting food or clothing, sending cards, or doing whatever else the situation calls for. To conclude the activity, students reflect on how it feels to get involved, what they learned from the experience, and how it was to work with their buddies.

Planning with Your Buddy Teacher

The impetus for doing this activity can come from the students, the two of you, or both; it can originate with the younger buddies or the older buddies. If something presents itself in the news or lives of your students and they are motivated to act, help them get organized. If you see a natural way to tap students' empathy and energy, take the lead.

Causes that interest your students may be related to a sudden disaster, such as an oil spill, neighborhood fire, flood, or earthquake, or they may spring from something your class is studying, such as a social studies focus on famine, a unit on children's lives in the midst of war, or a short story about a homeless family.

Well before a topic gets discussed with students, discuss in general what kinds of projects your classes might do and how the two of you want your classes to work together. This will be a whole-class pairing, not strictly a buddy pairing. Later, when a cause has been identified, talk about specific ways the classes can work together and how to let students take responsibility. Also talk about the possibility of the project going schoolwide and how you might communicate about it with the rest of the staff.

The most important planning you do will be in responding to students' goals and ideas – in helping them shape their involvement so that they feel a genuine commitment to making a difference.

Introducing the Activity with Older Students When They Take the Lead

- **Talk about the issue.** Facilitate a discussion of the issue at hand and the need for help. Invite students to share what they know about the situation and how it has affected people. Bring in relevant newspaper or magazine articles and invite students to do the same.

- **Host a special visitor or "expert" (optional).** Depending on the issue, you may want to invite a guest – such as an American Red Cross worker if you are helping with hurricane recovery, or someone from a social service agency if you are working on local homelessness. Invite the buddy class and let children sit with their buddies.

- **Have students brainstorm how they could help.** As students share their ideas, list them on the board. Review the list, helping students make the suggestions specific, eliminate those that are impractical, and choose the ones they will focus on.

- **Introduce the idea of working with younger buddies.** Invite students' ideas about how to include their buddies. What specific ways can the buddies help? What can the older students do to make sure the younger students feel responsible? What can they do so the younger students do not feel bossed around?

- **Arrange for the buddy class to consider participating.** Describe the proposed activity to your buddy teacher. Decide whether the buddy teacher or members of your class will introduce the idea to the younger students.

Introducing the Activity with Younger Students When They Take the Lead

- **Talk about the issue.** Facilitate a discussion about the issue and help students understand how it has affected people, particularly children. Encourage them to share what they know or what they're curious about.

- **Host a special visitor or "expert" (optional).** Invite a special guest who can make the issue more concrete for children. Include your buddy class and let children sit with their buddies.

- **Have students brainstorm how they could help.** Have the children share ideas about how they could help the people who are suffering. List their ideas on the board and then have the class discuss which ideas it might be possible for them to carry out.

- **Discuss sharing this activity with buddies.** Ask students to imagine working on this project with their buddies. What could the younger students do? What could the older students do? What could they do together?

- **Arrange for the buddy class to consider participating.** Describe the proposed activity to your buddy teacher. Decide whether the buddy teacher or members of your class will introduce the idea to the older students.

b-mail

This is an activity for whole-class b-mail. Have the initiating class send their buddy class an invitation to join them in working for a particular cause. As the activity proceeds, have both classes send each other mail describing ideas they're excited about trying, their assessments of how things are going, and ways they may want to change their plans.

Doing the Activity

- **Help students get organized.** Turn over as many details to the students as possible. Monitor their progress without taking over.

- **Hold joint and separate class meetings.** If the activity will extend over several weeks, hold regular meetings to assess how things are going with both the project and the buddies. Have students, in their separate classes and with the classes together, reflect on their goals, processes, and behaviors. What are they learning? What do they want to change or improve?

- **Observe and facilitate.** Depending on the scope of the activity, as you observe and facilitate you may also want to take photographs of the buddy classes making a difference together. Students are likely to feel proud of their efforts and contributions and may appreciate visual documentation for a scrapbook, hallway display, or their buddy journals.

Buddy Journals

With an ongoing activity, the cumulative entries in the buddy journals can be especially rich in narrative and reflection. At the conclusion of the activity, classes may want to compile a buddies' book about their experience, to which individual students contribute quotes from their journals.

Reflecting

In addition to the class meetings you hold during the activity, when the project is complete have students take a long view of the whole project. How did it feel to participate? What have they learned about the issue? Themselves? Their buddies? How might they do it differently next time?

With your buddy teacher, in addition to the ongoing meetings the two of you will have during the activity, have an end-of-the project evaluation and celebration. Discuss what went well and what was challenging. Give yourselves credit for helping your students lend a hand and make a difference.

Ways of Working for a Cause

Note: You may choose to present the ideas below as options for students to choose from or add to. If your students are responding to a local and immediate need, they may have ideas specific to that situation.

■ **Fundraisers Are Fun.** Together, the buddy classes plan and sponsor a fundraiser, such as a popcorn sale, a recycling drive, or a walkathon. In some way or another, these activities involve the entire school. If possible, help students see their gift in terms of tangible goods/services (books, meals, medicines) rather than money.

■ **Caring Cards.** Buddies work together to make cards for children in a hospital setting or who have been affected by a disaster. If the children's focus is a school that has been damaged or destroyed, they may want to accompany their cards with something special from their own classroom, or with original artwork, books they have written, or other handmade projects.

■ **Food/Clothing Drive.** For this kind of ongoing drive, the two buddy classes organize the details and invite the rest of the school (and community at large) to participate. Students make flyers, schoolwide announcements, and other requests for support — all of which emphasize helping, rather than competing for the most donations. A special drop-off point is established with the help of the custodial staff, and a process is arranged for transporting the goods to the appropriate agency.

Such a drive could also be organized as an Adopt-a-Family activity and coordinated with a local social service agency.

Materials

- Materials will vary with the activity
- Scrapbook or poster board for a display about the effort
- Camera (optional)

CELEBRATING OUR YEAR

AS THE END of the year approaches, buddies will want
to do something special to celebrate and appreciate
each other. The activities that follow are examples of ways
to do this — by helping students reflect on what they have
learned together throughout the year and by helping them
say "thanks" and show their mutual appreciation.
It couldn't hurt to combine either one with a
fun-filled picnic afternoon to
celebrate the year!

- **Celebrating Buddy Journals**
- **Thanking Our Buddies**

Celebrating Buddy Journals

By the end of the year, buddies will have looked back through their journals or portfolios many times, pointing out favorite drawings and ideas, reminding each other of favorite times, maybe even remembering some things that didn't go well or some things they've gotten better at. For this final journal activity of the year, buddies do a more formal kind of browsing—they mine the data in their journals to help them answer some questions about themselves as learners and friends.

The journal investigation and synthesis that buddies do together can help them appreciate the significance of a long-term commitment to a project or relationship. It will also give them practice for sharing the journals with someone at home.

Activity Structure

In their separate classes, students first brainstorm ideas about how the buddies benefited from their year together and then make individual lists of the benefits they found personally important. During Buddies time, the pairs look through their journals for specific evidence of these benefits. To extend or simplify the activity, the buddies could choose some special pages to tell another pair of buddies about and buddy foursomes could browse through the journals and exchange stories.

Planning with Your Buddy Teacher

Decide how structured you want to make the sharing time. Buddies could have an ambitious list or only a few straightforward questions to investigate. They could choose one or two pages to share with another buddy pair or they could informally browse each other's entire journals. Decide whether the celebration of the journals will be accompanied by refreshments and a ceremony. Review the steps described below and make adjustments depending on your particular decisions.

Note: If buddies have been sharing a looseleaf journal, the creation of the second journal for each pair should be handled as a separate activity, previous to this meeting. To create a second journal for each pair, photocopy all the journal pages. The buddy pairs then make a second cover and decide which original and which photocopied pages go in each journal.

Introducing the Activity with Older Students

- **Explain the purpose of the activity.** Tell students that they will have a chance to review their journals with their buddies as a way to remember their year and think about what they enjoyed and accomplished together.

- **Have students brainstorm a list of the benefits of their buddy experience.** Structure the brainstorm for students as a Venn diagram with the categories: "How did I benefit from working with my buddy over the year?" and "How did my buddy benefit from working with me?" You might have students work first with a partner to brainstorm specific benefits, and then bring the whole group back together. Record students' ideas on the board.

- **Have students make "detective lists."** From the brainstorm lists, have students choose some ideas that are most important to them personally and write them down. These lists will be the "detective lists" that students share with their younger buddies. Explain that the buddies will look through their buddy journals for evidence of the ideas on the detective list. For example, if a student writes on his or her detective list that "learning patience" and "acting out role-plays" were important benefits of being buddies, then with his or her buddy, the two will go through their journals looking for evidence or memories of times when either of them was patient or times when they role-played together. Tell students that their younger buddy will also have a detective list, of a simpler sort.

Introducing the Activity with Younger Students

- **Explain the purpose of reviewing the buddy journals.** Discuss why people keep journals or scrapbooks. Ask why people like to look at them over and over. Explain that students will have one last time to look at their buddy journals with their buddies before they take their journals home.

- **Have students consider a list of questions about their buddy times.** Have students brainstorm questions to add to the following: Which time was most fun? What was my favorite thing to learn? What was my buddy's favorite thing to learn? Which time did I try the hardest? Which time did my buddy help me the most? What is something I will remember about my buddy? What is something my buddy will remember about me?

- **Compile a list of students' questions.** Make a photocopy for each student.

- **Have students star their favorite questions.** Explain that when the students get together with their older buddies, they will look through their journals and choose the journal pages that answer the starred questions on their list. Tell students that their older buddies will have some questions, too.

b-mail

Invite buddies to send each other a "preview" question that they will investigate together.

Doing the Activity

- **Give buddies time to go over both sets of questions.** Before distributing the journals, have buddies talk a little together about the questions or detective list each has brought. Have them decide how to structure their investigation so that both buddies' questions get answered.

- **Encourage browsing as well as investigation.** When pairs have finished their investigations, encourage them to browse through their journals together, as well as to share them with other buddy pairs.

- **Have buddies reflect on their experience.** Ask children what they enjoyed about going over their journals. Ask them what kinds of things they will talk about when they share their journal with someone at home.

Buddy Journals

Invite buddies to make their final journal entry. Let buddies autograph each other's journals. Encourage them to draw pictures or write notes that express their thanks for the year together.

Reflecting

With your separate classes, invite students to talk about what they have learned this year about being buddies. What was hard? What was enjoyable? What was valuable?

With your buddy teacher, do your own review of the year. How did your students benefit? How did each of you benefit? What would you do again? What would you change?

Materials

- Two journals for each buddy pair
- Detective lists for older buddies
- Starred question lists for younger buddies
- Supplies for writing and drawing autographs

Thanking Our Buddies

Thanking Our Buddies is a flexible, end-of-the-year activity to allow buddies to thank each other, show their appreciation, and celebrate their friendship. Rather than letting the buddy relationships slip away unremarked with the end of the school year, this activity punctuates and adds special meaning to the whole Buddies experience.

Thanking Our Buddies turns an inevitable ending or goodbye into an opportunity for reflection and sharing. Whether students exchange handmade cards or whole-class songs, this activity includes everyone in showing appreciation and feeling appreciated.

Activity Structure

In their separate classes, older and younger students decide on one or more ways to thank and show appreciation for their buddies. Some of the activities can be from one class to another, but at least one expression of thanks should come from each child to his or her individual buddy. In class, students have time to plan and work on their Thanking Our Buddies projects. During Buddies time, children make their presentations, share any remaining reflections on the year, and have a little fun together.

Planning with Your Buddy Teacher

Before gathering activity suggestions from your students, share ideas about Thanking Our Buddies activities you both agree would be appropriate and manageable. (Some ideas are provided in "Ways of Thanking Our Buddies," below.) Decide on a general structure — will students exchange personal thank-yous only or whole-class thanks as well? Agree on a way the two of you will model saying thank you. Decide whether to have buddies celebrate with food and other festive touches. Your shared understandings will help you guide students' discussions of ways to thank their buddies. Review the steps described below and make adjustments as needed.

Introducing the Activity with Older Students

- **Talk about saying goodbye.** Bring out photographs, buddy journals, and other mementos of the time spent with buddies over the year. Describe how you're feeling about remembering the year and saying goodbye. Invite students to talk with a partner and then share some of their feelings with the rest of the class.

- **Have students brainstorm ways to thank their buddies.** Talk about ways students can say thank you personally to their buddies and ways the whole class can say thank you to the buddy class. List students' suggestions on the board.

- **Have students decide on a plan.** As a class, decide on a project everyone can work on individually and something special for the whole class to do. Talk about presentation. If students are writing something, would they like to read it aloud to their buddy? If the class is performing a song, how will that go?

- **Provide in-class time.** Let students work on and practice their individual and whole-class projects in class. Prepare your own thank-you and be available to lend students a hand.

Introducing the Activity with Younger Students

- **Talk about saying goodbye.** Let students know that it will soon be time to say goodbye to their buddies. Have them talk about other times when they have said goodbye and how such times may be similar to or different from saying goodbye to their buddy.

- **Have students remember their buddy year.** Invite students to remember some of the things they have done with their buddies. Show photographs and bring out some of the buddy projects. Have students discuss what they have enjoyed and what they have learned from their buddies.

- **Discuss some ways they could thank their buddies.** Invite students' suggestions. Point out that some ideas are better for the whole class to do and some are better for students to do individually.

- **Decide on two activities.** Decide on a project for everyone to work on individually for his or her own buddy, and one special thank-you from the whole class.

- **Give students class time to prepare individual thank-yous.** Encourage the sharing of ideas and materials. Prepare your own thank-you.

- **Prepare a whole-class thank-you.** Help students work together on a whole-class thank-you to their buddy class.

b-mail

Have the buddy classes send each other invitations to get together and "Remember When."

Doing the Activity

- **Give buddies time to exchange their personal thank-yous.** Circulate and participate as appropriate. Thank your buddy teacher.

- **Present the whole-class thank-yous.** One of you may want to emcee.

- **Other festivities (optional).** This may be a natural time to include pizza or ice cream, a picnic, or other treats that are fun for everyone.

Buddy Journals

If the journals have not yet been sent home (see "Celebrating Buddy Journals" on page 125), have students describe their buddy thank-yous in words or pictures.

Reflecting with Your Buddy Teacher

Congratulations — you've made it through an entire year. Unless you already did this as part of Celebrating Buddy Journals, plan a time to sit back and reflect on your experience. Share your thoughts about what went really well, what you learned, how you feel about the challenges that came up, and what the students got out of it all. Make a record of anything that might be important in the future to you or others.

Ways of Thanking Our Buddies

- **Remember When.** Individually, buddies write or draw their memories of the funny, interesting, difficult, and rewarding things they did with their buddy. Or, the whole class could devise a skit, song, or poem based on "Remember When."

- **What I've Learned from You.** Students think about what they've learned from their individual buddies during the year, and then express it in a poem, drawing, card, or whatever form they come up with. This activity is surprisingly powerful for older buddies, as they think about what they've learned from the younger ones. Another option is to do a whole-class "What We've Learned from You" project. For this, students could create a banner, mural, song, choral poem, or even a short play.

- **My, How You've Grown.** For this activity, each older student reflects on the ways his or her little buddy has changed and grown over the year. Students make some notes, share their thoughts with a partner, and then come up with a card or poem to let their buddy know. For younger children, it's a wonderful treat to share in an older buddy's reflections and positive insights about them.

- **Thanks in a Song.** As a class, students write and practice a song about their Buddies year. The lyrics can be funny or serious, rhymed or not, set to an original or familiar tune, and the presentation can be pantomimed, costumed, or danced to.

Materials

- Photographs, journals, and mementos from the buddy year
- Art supplies for making cards and drawings
- Costumes (optional)
- Musical instruments (optional)

PART 5

Resources

- Goal Setting for Teacher Partnerships
- Buddies Activity Assessment
- Sample Letter Home
- Class Reflection Guide

Goal Setting for Teacher Partnerships

With your buddy teacher, take turns interviewing each other. Use the questions below and make notes so that after the interviews you can compare your ideas and discuss particular points of interest.

Think of a time from your childhood or your teaching career when a cross-grade experience turned out very well. What were the contributing factors?

What do you hope your children get out of Buddies this year?

What do you hope to get out of Buddies?

Which aspects of Buddies do you feel most comfortable with?

Think of a time from your childhood or your teaching career when a cross-grade experience turned out very badly. What were the contributing factors?

Which aspects of Buddies are you most worried about and why?

What things are most important to you in working with a partner?

Which of your interests or skills might be useful in our Buddies program?

Buddies Activity Assessment

The following assessment guide is designed to help you plan activities that are both meaningful and fun—activities that reinforce your goals for students. Feel free to make as many copies as you need.

ACTIVITY NAME: _____

Does the activity promote positive social values?

Take stock of the specific values this activity will promote and those that it won't promote. Also keep in mind that activities designed to promote positive values can sometimes have unanticipated negative effects.

Does the activity foster

- ☐ cooperation?
- ☐ responsibility?
- ☐ caring?
- ☐ helpfulness?
- ☐ interpersonal understanding?
- ☐ appreciation of differences?

Does the activity avoid

- ☐ fostering unhealthy competitiveness?
- ☐ undermining self-esteem?
- ☐ encouraging disrespect?
- ☐ focusing too much on the product?

Does the activity contribute to a learning orientation?

Although many buddy activities have a primary focus on building relationships and promoting positive social values, the activities should also be consistent with, and in most cases support, academic goals as well.

- ☐ Is the activity consistent with our learning goals for students?

- ☐ Are older children as well as younger children learning—either by teaching or because the activity is structured to engage both age groups?

- ☐ Do children have opportunities to make connections between what they are learning and their prior knowledge and experiences?

- ☐ Do children have opportunities to share what they are learning with others, such as parents or other students?

Is the activity appropriate for younger buddies and older buddies?
Students of different ages can participate in the same activity and learn different things as a result. An opportunity for younger children to practice reading skills, for example, may also be an opportunity for older children to learn to teach with patience and kindness. The buddies need not be learning the same thing, but the activity should be meaningful and comfortable for both of them.

Does the activity offer older buddies an opportunity to
- [ ] share what they know?
- [ ] practice teaching?
- [ ] learn something new?
- [ ] be a caring friend?
- [ ] have fun?
- [ ] act as a role model?
- [ ] make some choices about how to work with their buddies?

Does the activity offer younger buddies an opportunity to
- [ ] get to know older buddies better?
- [ ] learn to do something they might not be able to learn on their own?
- [ ] make some choices?
- [ ] share what they're learning with others?

Does the activity avoid making either buddy feel
- [ ] left out or unimportant?
- [ ] frustrated by the difficulty level?
- [ ] competitive with other buddy pairs?

Is the activity manageable?
With so many demands on your time, it's important to choose buddy activities that are manageable. Keep in mind that what matters most is the experience children have together, not the product they make.

Does the activity
- [ ] require a reasonable level of teacher time and energy?
- [ ] require a reasonable amount of classroom buddy time?
- [ ] require resources you have or can obtain?

Are there potential adaptations for this activity?
Before discarding a favorite activity that may have some shortcomings, see whether it can be altered to better meet your goals for buddy activities.

Sample Letter Home

We encourage you to take the time to write a brief letter to parents and families to let them know about Buddies. The more families know about your goals at school, the more you can work together in mutually supportive ways. You might encourage parents to ask their children about Buddies, to share stories about older and younger friends they've had in their own lives, and to visit the classroom during Buddies time.

The note below is only a sample. Borrow from it whatever is useful as you create your own personal message home.

....

Dear Family Members and Family Friends,

This year we are again working especially hard to help the children feel comfortable and cared for at school. We hope to make our school community feel even more like an "extended family," and we invite all of you to join us and participate in making this happen.

I'm writing today to let you know about our Buddies program—a program that will allow every child in our class to develop a special friendship with a buddy from the _____ grade. The older students will be helping the younger children with a variety of learning activities, and we'll also be doing special things such as having lunch together now and then and attending assemblies together.

We hope and expect that the children will get a lot out of the experience. Buddies provides an excellent opportunity for older children to be caring helpers, teachers, and friends. Younger children can benefit from having a role model and a special, older friend at school.

You may want to ask your child about Buddies, particularly on _____, the day we will meet each week. Don't worry that you may not know the specific activity for the day—just ask an open-ended question such as "How did it go with your buddy today," and let your child fill you in. The buddy friendships turn out to be very important to children. Your interest in this relationship will only make it more valuable. Thanks for your participation!

Yours truly,

Estimados padres, familiares o amigos:

Este año estamos volviendo a hacer un esfuerzo especial para que los niños se sientan bien y a gusto en la escuela. Esperamos crear un ambiente familiar en nuestra comunidad escolar, y les invitamos a todos ustedes a participar en esta labor.

Les escribo hoy para darles a conocer nuestro programa de "Buddies" o "Compañeros especiales". Este programa permitirá que cada niño y niña en nuestro salón desarrolle una amistad especial con alguien del _____ grado. Los niños mayores ayudarán a los niños más pequeños con una serie de actividades de aprendizaje. También tendremos algunas ocasiones especiales donde, por ejemplo, almorzaremos juntos o asistiremos juntos a una asamblea.

Esperamos que los niños aprendan mucho de estas experiencias. Serán una excelente oportunidad para que los niños mayores ejerciten el papel de ayudantes, maestros y maestras, y amigos, mientras que los más pequeños se beneficiarán al tener amigos mayores en la escuela que les sirvan de ejemplo y de modelo.

Quizá querrá preguntarle a su hijo o a su hija sobre su nueva amistad. Estaremos reuniéndonos con nuestros compañeros cada _____. No se preocupe de no saber qué actividad se llevó a cabo ese día. Si le hace una pregunta abierta a su hijo o a su hija, como por ejemplo, "¿Qué tal te fue hoy con tu compañero especial o con tu compañera especial?", él o ella le contará a Ud. el resto. Estas amistades les resultan muy importantes a los niños. El interés que Ud. le dé la hará aún más valiosa.

Atentamente,

Class Reflection Guide

Making time for reflection need not be a burden. Reflection can be as simple as asking students "How did it go today?" and then being open to what they offer. What follows are a few discussion suggestions. Have students sometimes reflect while the buddies are still together, and sometimes when they are back in their regular class configurations.

General Discussion Time

Lead a class discussion about Buddies with your students, or have them talk first with a partner and then perhaps share with the whole class. Consider the following questions:

- How did it go today?

- What went well today with your buddy?

    How did it make you feel?

    How do you think your buddy felt?

- What, if anything, was difficult about working with your buddy today?

    How did it make you feel?

    How do you think your buddy felt?

As issues come up, invite students to work on problems with their classmates. You may want to begin with the following questions:

- Does anyone have any suggestions for how _____ might try to improve things?

- Is there anything I can do to help _____ out?

Teacher Support Materials from Developmental Studies Center

Now available

At Home in Our Schools. A 136-page guide to whole-school activities that help educators and parents create caring school communities. The guide includes ideas about leadership, step-by-step guidelines for 15 activities, and reproducible planning resources and suggestions for teachers.

At Home in Our Schools Videotape. A 12-minute video for use in staff meetings and PTO/parent gatherings to create support for a program of whole-school activities that build community. The documentary footage shows diverse schools using community-building activities.

Homeside Activities Books (Grades K–5). Six separate collections of activities that help teachers, parents, and children communicate. Each collection has an introductory overview, 18 reproducible take-home activities in English and Spanish, and suggestions for teachers on integrating the activities into the life of the classroom.

Homeside Activities Videotape. A 12-minute video for use at parent gatherings and staff meetings as an overview of a program of Homeside Activities. The documentary footage shows a range of classroom grades and home settings.

Reading, Thinking & Caring: Literature-Based Reading (Grades K–3). A children's literature program to help students love to read, think deeply and critically, and care about how they treat themselves and others. Teaching units are available for over 80 classic, contemporary, and multicultural titles. Each 3- to 10-day unit includes a take-home activity in English and Spanish to involve parents in their children's life at school. Complete grade-level sets, individual teaching units, and accompanying trade books are all available.

Reading for Real: Literature-Based Reading (Grades 4–8). A literature-based program to engage students' consciences while providing interesting and important reading, writing, speaking, and listening experiences. Teaching units are available for over 100 classic, contemporary, and multicultural titles, and each 1- to 3-week unit includes a take-home activity to involve parents in their children's life at school. Teachers report that this program engages even reluctant readers and builds community in the classroom. Complete grade-level sets, individual teaching units, orientation videotape, and accompanying trade books are all available.

Classroom Discussion: Collegial Study for Teachers. Videotaped segments from 13 literature-based discussions in *Reading for Real* classrooms presented on five cassettes: "Reflecting and Setting Goals," "Responding to Students," "Handling Offensive Comments and Sensitive Topics," "Guiding Students' Partner Discussions," and "Assessing Student Progress." Cassettes are available individually or as a set; the tapes and accompanying self-study guide can be used by partners, small groups, or individuals.

Number Power: Teacher Resource Books (Grades K–6). Seven separate *Number Power* books (one per grade), each offering three replacement units (8–12 lessons per unit) that foster students' mathematical and social development. Students collaboratively investigate problems, develop their number sense, enhance their mathematical reasoning and communication skills, and learn to work together effectively.

Number Power: Teacher Resource Packages (Grades K–6). Grade-level boxed collections of ready-to-use transparencies, die-cut manipulatives, blackline masters, and pads of group record sheets.

Choosing Community: Classroom Strategies for Learning and Caring. Nine videotaped presentations in which author and lecturer Alfie Kohn describes pivotal choices that promote community and avoid coercion and competition in classrooms. A facilitator's guide for use in staff development accompanies the presentations, which are available on four 43- to 60-minute cassettes, separately or as a set; the set includes Kohn's latest book, *Punished by Rewards: The Trouble with Gold Stars, Incentive Plans, A's, Praise, and Other Bribes.*

Ways We Want Our Class To Be: Class Meetings That Build Commitment to Kindness and Learning. Class meetings can be used to address academic and social issues that arise in the daily life of the elementary school classroom and to build a caring classroom community. This guide includes tips on getting started, ground rules, and facilitating the meetings, as well as 14 detailed guidelines for class meetings on specific topics in the categories of planning and decision making, checking in on learning and behavior, and problem solving.

That's My Buddy! Friendship and Learning Across the Grades. Whether for a whole-school program of cross-grade buddies or for two cooperating classrooms, this book is a practical guide that draws on the experiences of teachers from DSC's Child Development Project schools across the country. Also *That's My Buddy!* overview video.

Coming Soon from Developmental Studies Center

Ways We Want Our Class To Be Staff Development Package. These videos document the use of class meetings in a wide range of grades and for a variety of purposes. Teacher interviews provide practical insights.

Classroom as Community: Collaborative Learning in Action. Visits to collaborative classrooms in American pilot schools of DSC's Child Development Project showcase reflective teachers and the various ways they use CDP cooperative learning to build classroom communities.

Structuring a Collaborative Classroom. This guide offers 30 cooperative learning formats that can be used over and over to structure a collaborative classroom, as well as more than 100 sample activities in a variety of content areas.

For ordering information:

Publications Department
Developmental Studies Center
2000 Embarcadero, Suite 305
Oakland, CA 94606-5300

☎ (800) 666-7270
   (510) 533-0213